"When you arise in the morning give thanks for the morning light, for your life and strength. Give thanks for your food, and the joy of living. If you see no reason for giving thanks, the fault lies with yourself . . ."

Tecumseh

DOUBTING

THOMAS...

DOUBTING

AMERICA

DOUBTING
THOMAS...
DOUBTING
AMERICA

THOMAS BAYUK

Cover design:
Jonathan Gicewicz
J.E.G. Design
info@jegdesign.com

'Cover photo by Henry Kielblock—check:
www.SceneOutdoors.biz

Library of Congress Control Number: 2007909547
ISBN: Hardcover   978-1-4363-0742-0
                   Softcover   978-1-4363-0741-3

This book was printed in the United States of America.

To order additional copies of this book, contact:
Xlibris Corporation
1-888-795-4274
www.Xlibris.com
Orders@Xlibris.com
46005

To Joyce:
A perfect wife—who can find her ?

She is far beyond the price of pearls.
Proverbs 31: 10.

Many women have done admirable things, but you surpass them all.
Proverbs 31: 29

Doubting Thomas . . . Doubting America" is an enlightening and uplifting narrative regarding the declining and doubtful existence of God for both the author and America. It takes you on a journey with candor, humor, humility and joy. Everyone who has seriously sought to know God personally will immediately identify with Tom's struggle to find the answer to this question, "could it be that God desires to have an intimate relationship with me?" Tom takes us along on his journey of struggle and doubt and describes the many amazing and serendipitous experiences that regularly occurred which erased his doubt and convinced him that the God he was seeking was indeed in hot pursuit of him all the while. You will hear of the countless episodes and events that Tom encountered which revealed to him the presence and provision of God in extraordinary ways. Whether it came as a lone tomato and onion sitting on the vine in the dead of winter or thousands of dollars arriving in the "nick of time", it became evident that the God he was pursuing was quite amazing.

Tom's spiritual quest brought him to this truth. To believe is to become convinced that God will reveal Himself to those who earnestly seek Him and that it is His joy to provide for His children, often in remarkable ways. Tom's eyes were opened to the wonder of God's love and to the creative ways His love was continually expressed in their lives. This knowledge has inspired and motivated him through his experience with multiple sclerosis and has been the passion that propelled him to write this book. It will also delve into the mystery and causes of our societies declining and sadly misguided path. An eye-opening and awakening chronicle of where we have come from and where we could go . . . if we choose.

PROLOGUE

Interesting to note that on September 10th 2001 it was and still is illegal to say a prayer in any public school in the United States. It is also interesting to note that on September 11th 2001 one could not find a school in the entire Country that was not saying prayers.

It is widely acknowledged and accepted that church attendance in this Country has been dwindling for years. As usual church attendance on September 10th 2001 was sparse. However, on September 11th 2001 our churches throughout this Country were overflowing with attendance.

Fr. John Corapi

So who is it that is legislating God out of our society ? It surely is NOT the American public.

America was founded by persecuted folks fed up with living under the constraints, unfairness and restrictions of what was basically a corrupt society. We were founded by simple people seeking freedom and justice for all. It was not just for the select and the elite but for all. Those forefathers were definitely not the privileged and influential of British society. Quite the contrary. Australia was founded by the dregs of society. Their founders were outcasts and criminals. Canada was a similar circumstance. All three of these countries were founded on the principles and values of the Ten Commandments. These three countries are the youngest and that is the only reason that they are singled out.

Some incredibly interesting points to ponder regarding our beloved United States of America.

1. AS YOU WALK UP THE STEPS TO THE BUILDING THAT HOUSES THE U. S. SUPREME COURT YOU CAN SEE NEAR

THE TOP OF THE BUILDING A ROW OF THE WORLD'S LAW GIVERS AND EACH ONE IS FACING ONE IN THE MIDDLE WHO IS FACING FORWARD WITH A FULL FRONTAL VIEW. IT IS MOSES AND HE IS HOLDING THE TEN COMMANDMENTS.

2. AS YOU ENTER THE SUPREME COURTROOM, THE TWO HUGE OAK DOORS HAVE THE TEN COMMANDMENTS ENGRAVED ON EACH LOWER PORTION OF EACH DOOR.

3. AS YOU SIT INSIDE THE COURTROOM, YOU CAN SEE THE WALL RIGHT ABOVE WHERE THE SUPREME COUT JUDGES SIT, A DISPLAY OF THE TEN COMMANDMENTS.

4. THERE ARE BIBLE VERSES ETCHED AND CHISELED IN STONE ALL OVER THE FEDERAL BUILDINGS AND MONUMENTS IN WASHINGTON D. C.

5. JAMES MADISON, THE FOURTH PRESIDENT, KNOWN AS THE "FATHER OF THE CONSTITUTION" MADE THE FOLLOWING STATEMENT . . . . "WE HAVE STAKED THE WHOLE OF ALL OUR POLITICAL INSTITUTIONS UPON THE CAPACITY OF MANKIND FOR SELF-GOVERNMENT, UPON THE CAPACITY OF EACH AND ALL OF US TO GOVERN OURSELVES, TO CONTROL OURSELVES ACCORDING TO THE TEN COMMANDMENTS OF GOD."

6. PATRICK HENRY, THAT PATRIOT AND FOUNDING FATHER OF OUR COUNTRY SAID ; "IT CANNOT BE EMPHASIZED TOO STRONGLY OR TOO OFTEN THAT THIS GREAT NATION WAS FOUNDED NOT BY RELIGIONISTS BUT BY CHRISTIANS, NOT ON RELIGIONS BUT ON THE GOSPEL OF JESUS CHRIST'.

7. EVERY SESSION OF CONGRESS BEGINS WITH A PRAYER BY A PAID PREACHER, WHOSE SALARY HAS BEEN PAID BY THE TAXPAYER SINCE 1777.

8. THOMAS JEFFERSON WORRIED THAT THE COURTS WOULD OVERSTEP THEIR AUTHORITY AND INSTEAD OF INTERPRETING THE LAW WOULD BEGIN MAKING LAW . . . AN OLIGARCHY . . . . THE RULE OF FEW OVER MANY.

Consider the accomplishments in the World these past two hundred years. During this time for the most part God was always considered throughout the World.

No one in all of history has ever had more of an impact on humanity than Jesus Christ. He did not choose the academics or the wealthy or the privileged. It certainly has become rather obvious why He did not do that. He chose uneducated, tough men. Some of which were nothing more than "Thugs". Peter chopped off the ear one of those attempting to arrest Jesus. Surely a striking similarity in how our country became great. The strength of America comes from the average "Joe", the average man in the street. So once again we see that the ways of the Lord are surely not the ways that we would think or expect. Those twelve men took a message and changed the World.

Our foundling fathers and America also changed the world. But in recent years we have forsaken the values and discipline that have made us the greatest Country the world has ever seen. We are so entangled with political correctness and the accumulation of "Stuff" that we have lost our common sense. Our "Hi-Tech" era is so sophisticated that we have fooled ourselves into believing that success is "Whoever Accumulates the Most Toys".

Our academia, our judges, our politicians and those politically correct have forgotten God, He is no longer in our equation. That and that alone is the root of our problems. Eighty four per-cent of the population believes in God but yet the powers that be are removing Him from society. Christianity teaches one to respect and love your neighbor . . . . So does every other major religion . . . How can that possibly be wrong ?

Our politically correct leaders and special interest groups have altered the values, discipline and respect of this country, sadly.

Never before in all of human history has there ever been a society or culture that did not have or search for God. As complex as humans can be, if they did not have a God they created one . . . or many. The Greeks, the Romans, the Native Americans, the list is endless and as long as humanity has existed.

Never before in human history has a country or culture accomplished what the United States of America has accomplished for itself and mankind in the past two hundred or so years.

Never before has a society or culture succeeded in removing God from their existence. The latest attempt to do this was put forth by the Communists after the second World War and it failed.

And alas who would ever have thought or believed that the latest attempt to do so would be perpetrated by our very own "Politically Correct" leaders. Those same leaders that just a few short years ago were suggesting and considering changing our National Anthem from the Star Spangled Banner to "God Bless America". Something of an oxymoron ? A verse from "God Bless

America" asks Him to "Shed His Grace on Thee" and He surely has. Now we lie in the midst of those that would forgo and sacrifice the values, respect and discipline that our forefathers established and defended to the death.

Ralph Waldo Emerson said: "It is easy in the World to live after the World's opinion ; It is easy in solitude to live after our own ; but the great man is he who in the midst of the crowd keeps with perfect sweetness the independence of solitude".

As in the classic movie "Cool Hand Luke", "What we have here is a failure to communicate" . . . . The American public (The Crowd) does not want God removed from society. However, we have two crowds, we also have the "In Crowd" the Politically Correct, the insiders. And they just do not possess that "Perfect Sweetness and Independence" that integrity requires to do the right thing.

The 84% crowd needless to say should prevail, however, they (We) do not. From our "Declaration of Independence" ; **We hold these truths to be self-evident:**

That all men are created equal; that they are endowed by their Creator with certain unalienable rights; that among these are life, liberty, and the pursuit of happiness; that, to secure these rights, governments are instituted among men, deriving their just powers from the consent of the governed;How then is it possible in our democracy for 84% of the population to be over ruled? Sadly, it all has to do with power, votes and our "Insider Crowd". "By the People and for People" has slipped away. The "Declaration of Independence" makes reference to God and our Creator several times. Those that perpetrate this removal of God from our society will ask; So who is God? The Constitution of the United States of America plainly acknowledges that He does in fact exist. It also plainly acknowledges that He is whoever one believes Him to be . . . . or not be,FREEDOM . . . . at it's best

Our first amendment guarantees our right to worship God as each of us sees fit. It does NOT guarantee the removal of God from our currency, our Pledge of Allegiance, from His proper place in our society for the last two hundred years and our future.

Principal Jody McLeod

This is a statement that was read over the PA system at the football game at Roane County High School, Kingston, Tennessee, by school Principal, Jody McLeod.

"It has always been the custom at Roane County High School football games, to say a prayer and play the National Anthem, to honor God and Country."

Due to a recent ruling by the Supreme Court, I am told that saying a Prayer is a violation of Federal Case Law. As I understand the law at this time, I can use this public facility to approve of sexual perversion and call it "an alternate lifestyle," and if someone is offended, that's OK.

I can use it to condone sexual promiscuity, by dispensing condoms and calling it, "safe sex." If someone is offended, that's OK.

I can even use this public facility to present the merits of killing an unborn baby as a "viable means of birth control." If someone is offended, no problem . . .

I can designate a school day as "Earth Day" and involve students in activities to worship religiously and praise the goddess "Mother Earth" and call it "ecology."

I can use literature, videos and presentations in the classroom that depicts people with strong, traditional Christian convictions as "simple minded" and "ignorant" and call it "enlightenment."

However, if anyone uses this facility to honor GOD and to ask HIM to Bless this event with safety and good sportsmanship, then Federal Case Law is violated.

This appears to be inconsistent at best, and at worst, diabolical. Apparently, we are to be tolerant of everything and anyone, except GOD and HIS Commandments.

Nevertheless, as a school principal, I frequently ask staff and students to abide by rules with which they do not necessarily agree. For me to do otherwise would be inconsistent at best, and at worst, hypocritical . . . I suffer from that affliction enough unintentionally. I certainly do not need to add an intentional transgression.

For this reason, I shall "Render unto Caesar that which is Caesar's," and refrain from praying at this time.

"However, if you feel inspired to honor, praise and thank GOD and ask HIM, in the name of JESUS, to Bless this event, please feel free to do so. As far as I know, that's not against the law—yet."

One by one, the people in the stands bowed their heads, held hands with one another and began to pray.

They prayed in the stands. They prayed in the team huddles. They prayed at the concession stand and they prayed in the Announcer's Box!

The only place they didn't pray was in the Supreme Court of the United States of America—the Seat of "Justice" in the "one nation, under GOD."

Somehow, Kingston, Tennessee remembered what so many have forgotten. We are given the Freedom OF Religion, not the Freedom FROM Religion. Praise GOD that HIS remnant remains!

JESUS said, "If you are ashamed of ME before men, then I will be ashamed of you before MY FATHER."

Amen!

A prayer given in Kansas at the opening session of their Senate. It seems prayer still upsets some people. When Minister Joe Wright was asked to open the new session Of the Kansas Senate, everyone was expecting the usual generalities, but this is what they heard:

"Heavenly Father, we come before you today to ask your forgiveness and to seek your direction and guidance. We know Your Word says, "Woe to those who call evil good", but that is exactly what we have done.

We have lost our spiritual equilibrium and reversed our values. We confess that.

We have ridiculed the absolute truth of Your Word and called it Pluralism.

We have exploited the poor and called it the lottery,

We have rewarded laziness and called it welfare,

We have killed our unborn and called it choice,

We have shot abortionists and called it justifiable,

We have neglected to discipline our children and called it building self-esteem,

We have abused power and called it politics,

We have coveted our neighbor's possessions and called it ambition,

We have polluted the air with profanity and pornography and called it freedom of expression,

We have ridiculed the time-honored values of our forefathers and called it enlightenment.

Search us, Oh, God, and know our hearts today; cleanse us from every sin and set us free. Guide and bless these men and women who have been sent to direct us to the center of Your will and to openly ask these things in the name of Your Son, the living Savior, Jesus Christ.

Amen!"

The response was immediate. A number of legislators walked out during the prayer in protest. In 6 short weeks, Central Christian Church, where Rev. Wright is pastor, logged more than 5,000 phone calls with only 47 of those calls responding negatively. The church is now receiving international requests for copies of this prayer from India, Africa, and Korea.

Commentator Paul Harvey aired this prayer on his radio program, "The Rest of the Story", and received a larger response to this program than any other he has ever aired.

With the Lord's help, may this prayer sweep over our nation and wholeheartedly become our desire so that we again can be called "one nation under God.

From our Native American Indians . . . .

O' GREAT SPIRIT,

WHOSE VOICE I HEAR IN THE WINDS;AND WHOSE BREATH GIVES LIFE TO ALL THE WORLD,HEAR ME !I AM SMALL AND WEAK, I NEED YOUR STRENGTH AND WISDOM. LET ME WALK IN BEAUTY, AND MAKE MY EYES EVER BEHOLD THE RED AND PURPLE SUNSET.

MAKE MY HANDS RESPECT THE THINGS YOU HAVE MADE AND MY EARS SHARP TO HEAR YOUR VOICE.

MAKE ME WISE SO THAT I UNDERSTAND THE THINGS YOU HAVE TAUGHT MY PEOPLE.

LET ME LEARN THE LESSONS YOU HAVE HIDDEN IN EVERY LEAF AND ROCK.

I SEEK STRENGTH, NOT TO BE GREATER THAN MY BROTHER, BUT TO FIGHT MY GREATEST ENEMY . . . MYSELF.

MAKE ME ALWAYS READY TO COME TO YOU WITH CLEAN HANDS AND STRAIGHT EYES.

SO WHEN LIFE FADES, AS THE FADING SUNSET, MY SPIRIT MAY COME TO YOU WITHOUT SHAME.

NBC News took a survey and found that eighty four per cent of the population believes in God and does NOT want "IN GOD WE TRUST" removed from our currency. That same citizenry does NOT want "ONE NATION UNDER GOD" removed from the "Pledge of Allegiance".

An open letter from Fr. John Corapi:

SIX YEARS LATER. THE APPROACH OF MIDNIGHT
BY REV. JOHN A. CORAPI

SIX YEARS AGO ON SEPTEMBER 11, 2001 TIME STOOD STILL IN A SPASMOF BLACK SMOKE, DEATH, AND DESTRUCTION. IT HAD NEVER HAPPENED BEFORE, BUT NOW IT HAD, PROVING DEFINITIVELY THAT IT COULD HAPPEN. AN ERA ENDED. INDEED, WE WOULD NEVER BE THE SAME.

FOR A TIME, IT SEEMED TO THOSE STILL POSSESSED OF ANY ABILITY TO SEE SPIRITUAL THINGS AT ALL THAT PERHAPS THE WORLD MIGHT CORRECT IT'S BLIND AND HEADLONG FLIGHT OVER A PRECIPICE AND INTO A MORAL ABYSS. PEOPLE RUSHED TO CHURCHES, SYNAGOGUES, AND MOSQUES. THERE WERE LONG LINES FOR CONFESSION IN THE CATHOLIC CHURCHES. OTHERS MADE THEIR AMENDS WITH GOD AND EACH OTHER IN WHATEVER WAY THEY COULD, NOT SURE WHAT WAS NEXT, NOT TAKING ANY CHANCES.

THE VERY HEART OF THE PORNOGRAPHY AND ABORTION INDUSTRIES SUFFERED A NEAR FATAL CASE OF CASH REGISTER ARREST. CLOSE PROXIMITY TO DEATH TENDS TO BRING REALITY INTO FOCUS.

TIME HEALS ALL THINGS, IT IS SAID. YES, AND IN THIS CASE EVEN MOMENTS OF MORAL LUCIDITY AND SPIRITUAL CLARITY WERE "HEALED" AND REPLACED BY BUSINESS AS USUAL. MANKIND HAS A SHORT MEMORY DESPITE THE CONSTANT REMINDERS OF HISTORY. IN THE SIX YEARS SINCE 911 HAS A SOCIETY CRIPPLED BY EASE, DEBILITATED BY POLITICAL CORRECTNESS, AND CLOSE TO DEATH FROM THE MORAL MALAISE THAT HAS PLAGUED IT FOR DECADES LEARNED ANYTHING?

APPARENTLY NOT, FOR TODAY EVEN MOST RELIGIOUS LEADERS ARE LOATH TO LINK 911 WITH THE REALITY OF SIN. THE WORD ITSELF HAS BEEN EXILED, MUCH LIKE GOD HIMSELF, FROM OUR SCHOOLS, OFTEN EVEN FROM CHURCHES, AND, INDEED, FROM OUR VERY CONSCIOUSNESS.

THE FACT IS THAT WE REAP WHAT WE SOW. WHAT GOES AROUND, COMES AROUND. THE GREATEST NATION ON THE EARTH HAS THE GREATEST MORAL RESPONSIBILITY. INDEED, "TO THE MAN GIVEN MUCH, MUCH WILL BE REQUIRED. TO THE MAN GIVEN MORE, MORE WILL BE REQUIRED." WE WERE

ENTRUSTED WITH THE WELFARE OF THE WORLD, AND ALL TOO OFTEN THE TRUST WAS BETRAYED. UNDER THE SPECIOUS PRETEXT OF FREEDOM-WHICH WAS REALLY LICENSE-WE BECAME PURVEYORS OF PORNOGRAPHY, ABORTION, GREED, DECEIT, MURDER AND MAYHEM.

THE CLOCK IS TICKING AND MIDNIGHT IS APPROACHING. ILLUMINATED BY THE FALSE LIGHT OF AFFLUENCE AND EASE, SUCCESS AND POWER, WE BECAME BLIND TO THE DARKNESS, AND YET MIDNIGHT APPROACHES, WITH ALL OF THE CERTAINTY OF TIME ITSELF.

HAVE WE LEARNED ANYTHING IN THE PAST SIX YEARS, OR ARE WE YET MORE BLIND, MORE DEAF, MORE STEEPED IN SIN? ACTIONS HAVE CONSEQNENCES. 911 WAS A WARNING SHOT FIRED OVER THE BOW OF A SICK SOCIETY. THE WARNING HAS GONE LARGELY UNHEEDED.

THE CLOCK IS TICKING. MIDNIGHT IS APPROACHING. PRAYER IS NOW THE ONLY THING THAT WILL AVAIL CHANGE, SO PRAY MY DEAR FRIENDS, PRAY LIKE YOUR LIFE AND THE LIFE OF ALL YOU HOLD DEAR IS AT STAKE. FOR IT IS, IT IS. GOD BLESS YOU AND PROTECT YOU AND YOURS, REV. JOHN CORAPISEPTEMBER 11, 2007SIX YEARS LATER, AND COUNTING

Our Washington politicians have many pressing issues to act upon but they simply and constantly just haggle like children to get their way and nothing is being accomplished. Truth is truth, like it or not. The Bible says; "They will see but will not see . . . . They will hear but not hear". This country has a myriad of issues that need attention and action. But alas, being on the right side is more important than doing the right thing. To get a meeting of the minds is damn near impossible.

We have created an "I'm OK . . . Your OK" society . . . . trouble is, it is not OK. There are in fact "Rights" and there are in fact "Wrongs". The values, integrity, discipline and respect that have made this country great are no longer practiced. The media thrives on witch-hunts and negatives that constantly occur in any society. Very little reporting occurs concerning the positive and good things that also occur in all societies. It simply does not cause the sensationalism that negatives do.

Our leaders have lost the courage to stand up and say the right thing. Whatever is politically correct must now be considered first, integrity and doing the right thing if it is considered at all must be politically correct . . . . no one can be offended. With our "Hi-Tech" expertise we now have computers that can write speeches that will offend no one. How preposterous is that ? Truth is truth, like it or not.

God has and continues to be legislated out of our society. Agree or disagree, He has been the foundation of our country and society. Our forefathers guaranteed our right to worship the God that each individual choose to worship. That has served us well for over two hundred years but that is slowly slipping away. And right along with it are our values, discipline, integrity and respect. Clarence Thomas of the United States Supreme Court often referred to "Natural Laws" during his confirmation hearings . . . . the press and some of those confirming him ridiculed and tried to make a mockery of those "Natural Laws". However, those natural laws do in fact exist and we all know it, even those that deny them. It just might not be "Politically Correct" to acknowledge them to those in denial.

Our quest to "Get it while the getting is good is destroying us." It is now commonplace for both parents to work leaving our children to be brought up by day-care and strangers. Is it any wonder what we are in trouble?

As always, History repeats itself, we are doing the same thing that they did two thousand years ago. Our founders fought and died for religious freedom. We are fortunate enough to be free to worship as we each see fit. However, "the powers that be" seem to be telling God to leave us, fortunately He won't. When we sing "GOD BLESS AMERICA" we sing . . . "GOD SHED HIS GRACE ON THEE" and He surely and certainly has answered us. Now sadly our illustrious and self driven leaders are bowing to the special interest groups that would remove God from all of public society. They would have us remove Him from our Money, from our Pledge of Allegiance and from our schools. Bear in mind that it is NOT the average citizen that desires this but small minority of special interest groups.

We are a free country but freedom has responsibility and that responsibility is to do the right thing. Thankfully, the right thing ALWAYS stands out. Whether or not we do it is another question. Rest assured if we do not . . . we will in fact lose our freedom.

INTRODUCTION

Tom Bayuk, (aka, "Doubting Thomas") has written his life story with candor, humor, humility and joy. Everyone who has seriously sought to know God personally will immediately identify with Tom's struggle to find the answer to this question, "could it be that God desires to have an intimate relationship with me?" Tom takes us along on his journey of struggle and doubt and describes the many amazing and serendipitous experiences that regularly occurred which erased his doubt and convinced him that the God he was seeking was indeed in hot pursuit of him all the while. You will hear of the countless episodes and events that Tom encountered which revealed to him the presence and provision of God in extraordinary ways. Whether it came as a lone tomato and onion sitting on the vine in the dead of winter or thousands of dollars arriving in the "nick of time", it became evident that the God he was pursuing was quite amazing.

Tom's spiritual quest brought him to this truth. To believe is to become convinced that God will reveal Himself to those who earnestly seek Him and that it is His joy to provide for His children, often in remarkable ways. Tom's eyes were opened to the wonder of God's love and to the creative ways His love was continually expressed in their lives. This knowledge has inspired and motivated him through his experience with multiple sclerosis and has been the passion that propelled him to write this book.

Tom's experiences mirror the need for each of us to face and overcome our battles with doubt and unbelief in order to live a life of confidence and trust in God's abundant love.

Tom's victories over doubt show us how this can be done, and is best summed up in the words of Tennyson's "In Memoriam":

> Perplexed in faith, but pure in deeds,
> At last he beat his music out.
> There lives more faith in honest doubt,
> Believe me, than in half the creeds.
>
> He fought his doubts and gathered strength
> He would not make his judgment blind;
> He faced the specters of the mind,
> And laid them; thus he came at length
>
> To find a stronger faith his own;
> And power was with him in the night
> Which makes the darkness and the light,
> And dwells not in the light alone.

Francis X. Huber
Pastor . . . First Christian Assembly, Plainfield, New Jersey

CONTENTS

AUTHOR'S NOTE

I have not had or led an extraordinary life by any means. However, I have certainly had more than my share of extraordinary occurrences . . . . "Just Falling into Place". A series of gripping and astonishing events spanning fifty years. Coincidences some might say, luck others may say. But the fact of the matter is that the puzzle of life fits so perfectly that it cannot be either of those. This book is about them and will compel the reader to question their own life, purpose and reason.

Nearly twenty three years ago I was diagnosed with multiple sclerosis. Prior to that time "I was not what one would have considered to be a humble man". I had always been a loud, proud, boisterous and extroverted individual. One day though on my way to work out at the gym, everything was changed forever. Interestingly and amazingly the changes that occurred were and are not negative and if anything have awoken my senses. That day is the day that made me "Stop, Look and Listen" to life, in spite of myself.

It is interesting to note that in this day and age the values that we have created for ourselves are measured by fortune, fame and status. It is also interesting to note that in order to achieve these goals we have been led, taught or programmed to believe that it is all within our grasp and control. For most of my life I was a most adamant and firm follower of that philosophy. In view of that and without question I am still a firm believer of the power and influence of positive thinking.

However, I now realize that the most crucial and missing ingredient in that philosophy is the awareness of God in our lives. Many have succeeded with fortune, with fame, with stardom, with status . . . . and still they search. Is that all there is ? No ! That is not all there is. The missing ingredient is the knowledge of knowing that God is with us and wants us to know Him. If we allow Him to come to us He will. He has given us a free will to choose . . . . and He gives us time and opportunity to make that choice. He is a most merciful

God and He longs for us to long for Him . . . . for our own sake. Who else could be that merciful ?? Our hearts are restless until they rest in God. Our human nature is such that we will not accept or believe anything until and unless we understand that something. However, we are entering into an area that we are not going to understand. It is beyond our comprehension and to think otherwise is nothing more than foolishness. Nevertheless, we do have another option and only one, that single option is Faith. If you are not sure of that or do not believe that, stop reading for a moment. Now say a simple prayer but be sincere and deliberate, it is possible to be a skeptic and sincere at the same time maybe even likely. If you were sincere there will be a peace or at the very least a hope. Just where did that peace or hope come from?

During World War I, this special prayer, known as "The Soldier's Prayer" was recited daily by each member of the 91st Brigade, The 91st Brigade was engaged in three of the bloodiest battles of the war; Chateau Thierry, Belieu Wood, and the Argonne Forest. While other units similarly engaged in these battles suffered up to ninety percent casualties, the 91st Brigade DID NOT SUFFER A SINGLE COMBAT-RELATED CASUALTY.

Psalm 91

He who dwells in the secret place of the most high
Shall abide under the shadow of the Almighty.
I will say of the Lord, "He is my refuge and my fortress:
My God, in Him I will trust."
Surely He shall deliver you from the snare of the fowler.
And from the perilous pestilence.
He shall cover you with his feathers.
And under His wings you shall take refuge:
His truth shall be your shield and buckler.
You shall not be afraid of the terror by night.
Nor of the arrow that flies by day.
Nor of the pestilence that walks in darkness.
Nor of the destruction that lays waste at noonday.
A thousand may fall at your side, and ten thousand at your right hand
But it shall not come near you.
Only with your eyes shall you look,
And see the reward of the wicked.
Because you have made the Lord, who is my refuge.
Even the Most High, your habitation.

No evil shall befall you.
Nor shall any plague come near your dwelling:
For He shall give His angels charge over you,
To keep you in all your ways.
They shall bear you up in their hands.
Lest you dash your foot against a stone.
You shall tread upon the lion and the cobra.
The young lion and the serpent you shall trample underfoot.
Because He has set His love upon Me. Therefore I will deliver him:
I will set him on high, because he has known My name.
He shall call upon ME, and I will answer him:
I will be with him in trouble;
I will deliver him and honor him.
With long life I will satisfy him,
And show him My salvation.

CHAPTER 1

In the beginning

Happy the man who discovers wisdom,
The man who gains discernment:
Gaining her is more rewarding than silver,
More profitable than gold.
She is beyond the price of pearls,
Nothing you could covet is her equal.

PROVERBS 3:13-15

Trust . . . a most interesting word. It means faith, belief, conviction, reliance, hope, confidence, expectation and all of those things put together. It is also one of the rarest, most coveted character traits that we could desire or possess. You can see it and feel it in a loving, happy marriage. You can see it and feel it between men that have been at war together. You can also see it and feel it in any human inter-action when all of the parties involved possess it. And lastly but most vital of all you can see it and feel it when one trusts in God. It just might be the most significant character trait due to the peace of mind that it provides to the one trusting.

My Mother was Catholic and my Father was Jewish. I am the youngest of three boys and we were raised Catholic. Every Sunday my Father would drop us off at St. Joseph's church in North Plainfield, N. J. After Mass I would have to go to Sunday school held in the church hall located beneath the church. I was five years old and hated it. The only thing that was good about that was my teacher Sister Kenneth, she was young, very pretty and kind. Two years later, I received my First Holy Communion.

I was an obstinate kid and would not wear short pants. All of the boys in the Sunday school class had to wear white suits for our First Holy Communion and the suits all had short pants. That was unacceptable to me and I refused to wear them.

My Father came to my rescue and took me to the Lower East Side in New York City. He took me to a tailor to have a white suit made for me with long pants. I wonder how he explained that to the Jewish tailor. Here we had a Jewish Father hiring a Jewish tailor to make a white Holy Communion suit for his Catholic son. Heh, heh.

I went to public school and up until eighth grade we were dismissed every Tuesday at 2:00 PM for religious classes. Religion was not one of my favorite subjects and very often instead of going to those classes I could be found at a local soda fountain playing the pinball machine. Be that as it may, somehow I was confirmed when I was fourteen years old.

From that time on I went to Church simply because my Mother made me go to Church. I never paid much attention to religion or being Catholic or Praying.

There was one exception and that exception is the first time that I remember ever really Praying to God of my own volition. When I was seventeen years old one of my best friends got me a date with his girl friend's twin sister. School had just been let out for the summer and I was about to begin my Senior year of high school the following September.

I really couldn't believe that this girl would even go out with me. She was very popular and also very beautiful. The entire junior and senior class boys were all dying to take her out. We really hit it off on that first date and continued to go out regularly for the next several weeks. I asked her to "Go Steady" on July 10, 1959 and she said yes. Talk about stunned, well I surely was, ecstatic as well.

That night is the first night that I Prayed to God . . . . "Dear God, please do not ever let anything stop or happen to Joyce and our relationship. Please watch over her, keep her safe and do not ever let anything come between us." There was a constant fear in the back of my mind that this would not last.

But it did last and we were married two years and nine months later. I was nineteen years old and she was eighteen. That was just about forty five years ago. And in all of that time there has never been a day of regret or unhappiness with each other. We have certainly had our share of "Bumps in the road" but nothing has ever come between us. I said that Prayer every single night for the next twenty five or thirty years. I still say a slight variation of that Prayer . . . . Lucky ?? . . . . Impossible. What could I have possibly known about life, about marriage, about anything at seventeen years of age ? Our marriage is a gift from God, there just cannot be any other explanation. Nothing else makes sense.

We have had a number of other circumstances in our lives that defy explanation. Most of my life I wasn't even sure if there was a God. I always wondered about things, how they came to be etc. but it seemed that there really were no definite answers. I think that I knew better but in actuality I did not want to know for sure.

It was always "My way or the highway" and I liked it like that. Spoiled . . . ? I suppose, it must have started with that white suit. Fortunately for me I had very loving and caring parents, to a fault . . . maybe. Growing up they owned a business so I had a lot of time on my own. That was fine and I liked calling my own shots and being in control of my free time. The only thing that interfered with that was God and Church. I did not like that interference, I liked my way better. My wife on the other hand always went to church on Sunday, willingly. The first few months that we were married I did too but eventually stopped going at all. We had three children by the time Joyce was twenty two and she was adamant about taking them to church.

So I started going back to church but my heart really was not in it. I just didn't get it. We even tried going to a Methodist church that a friend of mine attended. That did not make any difference to me and slowly but surely I stopped going to church again.

However, I did think that it was important for the kids to go so we went back to the Catholic Church. Actually, I should say that Joyce and the kids went back, I dropped them off and picked them up. Sadly through no fault of anyone other than myself, it has taken me most of my life to learn and understand the Catholic Church.

The first fifteen hundred years after Christ's crucifixion there was only one church, the church that Jesus himself created, the Catholic Church. The authoritative teachings, discipline and guidelines were spoken by He alone. His follower's and successors did their very best to maintain those teachings and did so during all of that time. Those teachings and disciplines became known as the Magisterial guidelines of the Catholic Church.

Then about five hundred years ago Martin Luther broke away from the church. There had been many injustices and corrupt individuals distorting the Magisterium of the church. No doubt this caused many well intentioned and some not so well intentioned people to go their own way and start new churches. Which did in fact happen. It also swung open the doors for anyone to pick and choose what suited them and discard what did not. This of course led to chaos regarding who is right, who is wrong etc.

A striking correlation currently exists in our present day American society. Just take a look at our own bickering and inaction that occurs everyday in political arenas in Washington D.C. The politicians all run amok simply due to the fact that they seek their own individual agenda. First and foremost they do what they know will get them the most votes. Secondly, they have succeeded to insure their own security. The "Booty" that they have created for themselves is obscene compared to the rest of society.

Many of our laws are so confusing and conflicting that they are impossible to interpret. We currently have laws that will punish a pregnant woman for smoking or drinking while pregnant. The law states that she is endangering the unborn child. We also have a law that states that the unborn child is not a child . . . . These are our leaders, folks.

The same circumstance exists within the traditional American family. Is it any wonder ? The stress and pressure of financial well being and so-called success is creating problems that are becoming insurmountable. Most husbands and wives now work. Children are being brought up by "Day care" providers. The strength of any society is in direct proportion to the strength of the family within that society. Taking responsibility for one's action or inaction, respect and discipline must be taught to our children and that begins at home. Parents are the guiding light of any society and they are losing and sacrificing their roles for the sake of gain. Grand parents are meant to be revered and respected, we are basically discarding and discounting them. We need to get them out of the way so we can succeed . . . . what a tragedy.

CHAPTER 2

Bumps in the road

Let the wise man listen and he will learn more, and the man of discernment will acquire the art of guidance.

Proverbs 1:5

During the early sixties I was having a variety odd but minor health problems. There were a lot of strange feelings and sensations that would suddenly appear and then just as suddenly disappear. I went to a doctor at a major medical center in New York City. The doctor was recommended by a doctor that my father knew. After he examined me and I explained my history, he said I had a virus and to go home and don't worry about it, just live your life. Well that was exactly what I wanted to hear and that is just what I did. I was 22 years of age and it sounded good to me. When he said that I had a virus he never mentioned multiple sclerosis. That was the best thing that he could have done for me. Smart doctor, just go home and don't worry about it.

Several years later I was buying a life insurance policy and was turned down. The doctor in NYC had reported that I had MS. That was quite a shock. I didn't even know what MS was, if anything I thought it was the end of my life. The life that I had expected.

My brother had a good friend that was very religious and he thought that it might help if we met. So we made arrangements to have dinner at a local restaurant. The dinner was on a Saturday night at Pfenninger's Hilltop Inn located in Flemington, N. J.

We arrived at the restaurant with my brother and his wife Gail. Fran Huber, my brother's friend and his wife Kathy were already seated at the table. We were all introduced to each other and we sat down to have a drink before dinner.

After the introductions, Fran Huber was talking, he knew that I was troubled about my health circumstances. One of the first things that he said was "Well you know that we are all sinners." As soon as he said that, the hair on the back of my neck went up and I thought to myself . . . "Oh my God what have I gotten myself into". The last thing that I needed was a born again religious zealot.

However, the evening actually turned out to be a very enjoyable experience. Fran Huber had a great sense of humor, as did his wife and we did not discuss religion at all. The one thing that he did say was that a Catholic priest was giving a talk at his Pentecostal church in December and asked, would I like to go? It was now October and I had plenty of time to get out of it so I said yes and we made it definite. It was scheduled to be on a Sunday night.

Well horrible horrors, I forgot all about it. Then one Sunday afternoon in December the phone rang and it was Fran Huber. "Hi Tom, how are you? I'll pick you up at 5:30." I couldn't believe it, no time to get out of it . . . . I said "OK."

We arrived at the church at about 6:00 PM. As we entered the church I was very annoyed at myself for getting into this situation . . . . I definitely did not want to be here. The church was full, everyone was singing, hands in the air, giving bear hugs to one another . . . . I just wanted to run. After a brief period of time things settled down and everyone was seated.

Fran and I sat in the middle of a pew in the back or the church. Father Orsini began to speak. He spoke for about twenty or thirty minutes. Everything that he said really struck me and I was listening intently. He then asked "If any of you have been touched by my words . . . please come down here to the foot of the stage". The congregation pews were at ground level and the speakers podium was up on a stage in the rear of the church.

I wanted to go but was embarrassed and was not going to get up. At that moment, Fran Huber grabbed my arm, we had been silent the whole time, and said "Come on I'll walk you down." I was flabbergasted but got up and walked down to the stage with Fran.

There were about fifteen or twenty people standing in front of the stage and Father Orsini began to speak to us. He asked if we were having trouble believing but wanted to . . . . "That was exactly where I was." As he spoke he was looking straight at me, eye to eye. He is up on this stage speaking to all these people but he was looking straight into my eyes. Then he starts walking down off the stage, comes right up to me, hugs me and says "There's no turning back now".

I'm in shock now and did not know what to say or do. A number of folks came up to this group with hugs, accolades and congratulations. Everyone was all excited and the singing and hugging started all over again. This went on for about a half hour or so. I was feeling quite perplexed and was anxious to leave.

We left and on the ride home Fran talked about the wonders of the Lord as I listened and tried to soak up what just transpired. He asked if I would like to join him at a men's morning prayer meeting the next day. I wasn't sure one way or the other. I had an interest but did want to get too involved and said "Maybe next time". I had a lot to think about, I was interested but at the same time I was somewhat concerned of that interest.

My brother lived next to a doctor who knew a neurosurgeon that was said to be one of the best in the country and he said that I should go to him. That is what I did and he said that I did not have MS. He said that I had a nerve in my neck that was being encroached by a deteriorating disc. There was a serious danger of the nerve being severely and permanently damaged. He said that he could solve the problem by removing the damaged disc and replacing it with a piece of bone from my hip and fusing the vertebrae in my neck. The doctor said that I would be in the hospital for about ten days. He also said that I might need a blood transfusion and I would be in bed for a few days.

The operation was scheduled for early on a Friday morning. I checked into the hospital on Thursday. I was in a room for four at Somerset Hospital in Somerville, N. J. That night unbeknownst to me Fran Huber came to visit me. It was about 7:00PM and all of the patients in my room had visitors as well. Fran came to Pray for me, he had oil to anoint me and he was going to do it now. Just as Fran entered my room a nurse came into the room and said that she had to take me for some sort of test.

Fran said to the nurse "It'll have to wait, I'm here to say some prayers for this man." The room was full of visitors for the other patients. I couldn't believe it, I was embarrassed, even ashamed . . . . I'm sorry to say. All of the other patients and their visitors and the nurse watched as Fran said some prayers and anointed me with oil. I didn't know then what I know now. Thank God for Fran and those prayers.

Dr. Culberson did the cervical lamenectomy to eliminate my problem the next morning. Much to everyone's surprise especially Dr. Culberson and myself, there were no blood transfusions necessary, no difficulties and I was released from the hospital the following Monday. Dr. Culberson said that my progress was quite incredible.

My recuperation was to last at home for about four weeks. There was now plenty of time to reflect on those prayers that were said the night before my surgery.

In my typical way I wondered was it the prayers or was I just lucky ? In any event I started to read the Bible and began with the Greek translation of the New Testament. It was much more descriptive and detailed than any of the others that I had seen. There was an abundance of time on my hands so I spent it reading the Bible every day for a few hours. The more that I read the more immersed and fascinated I became with it.

As the weeks went by I was also reading the Old Testament and stumbled on several verses in "Genesis" that really astounded me. Genesis 9:12-15 . . . God said, "Here is the sign of the Covenant that I make between myself and you and every living creature with you for all generations: I set my bow in the clouds and it shall be a sign of the Covenant between me and the earth. When I gather the clouds over the earth and the bow appears in the clouds, I will recall the Covenant between myself and you and every living creature of every kind. And so the waters shall never again become a flood to destroy all things of flesh. When the bow is in the clouds I shall see it and call to mind the lasting Covenant between God and every living creature of every kind that is found on the earth."

For me theses verses were the very first words of the Bible that truly had an impact on my Faith or lack of it. Could it be that God was in fact communicating with us by way of the rainbow ? . . . . I thought so and hoped so. Twenty six years later I found that to be precisely and definitely so.

During that month or so we also became quite friendly with Fran and Cathy Huber. So much so that we all began going to his church, the First Pentecostal Assembly located in Plainfield, N. J. That was about thirty miles away and took between a half hour and forty five minutes to get there. This time I even began going to church, sometimes twice a week.

It was somewhat uncomfortable for me with all of that singing, hands in the air, praise the Lord this and praise the Lord that. However, my reading of the Bible had me significantly engrossed to keep on keeping on.

The recuperation from the operation was between four and six weeks. However, after three weeks I felt fine but still could not go back to work yet. We owned a luncheonette in Flemington, N. J. The doctor would not allow me back due to the bending, lifting, etc. But I felt fine, I was driving and could do everything but work. I had my real estate license and my brother had a real estate office in Clinton, N. J. We also lived in Clinton so I decided to sell real estate for the duration of my recuperation.

One night I went down to the office to make some calls to people that I knew that were financially capable of investing in real estate. Hunterdon County, N. J. was booming at the time. The Federal Government was building the Interstate Highway System and Interstate 78 was almost complete and had two interchanges in Clinton. I78 is a major East-West route that goes directly to New York City. That was the primary reason for the real estate boom.

A number of years back, I had worked for a very wealthy young business man named Jerry Dresner. So I called him hoping that he might be interested in investing in some real estate. The phone rang and a little kid answered. I asked if Jerry was there . . . and click, the kid hung up on me. So I called back and this time a woman answered. I asked for Jerry and she asked who was calling. I told her who I was and she said "Jerry Died". I was shocked and was now attempting to simply end the conversation.

I said how surprised and sorry that I was to hear this news and was sorry to disturb her. She asked why I called and told her it had to do with real estate. She said "Well just a minute, my Father-in-law is here and we were just discussing real estate", with that she handed the phone to Jerry's Father.

After I apologized and expressed my sympathy, etc. he said that they had a one hundred and eight acre parcel of real estate that they wanted to sell. It was land that was going to be used to expand their business but Jerry died. He told me where the property was located and that they wanted $5,000. per acre. He also said that if I sold it they would pay a ten per cent commission. We cordially ended the call and I said that I would get back to him in the next day or so.

I went to look at the property the next morning. It was located in Hillsborough Township, N. J. I did not know a heck of a lot about real estate but when I saw this land I couldn't believe my eyes. It was farmland and was situated in the midst of some extremely active real estate development. The property had over a mile of road frontage. It also had two railroad tracks running through it. The Lehigh Valley Railroad and the Central Railroad of New Jersey. About half of the land was zoned light industry and the other half, the land between the two railroads was zoned heavy industrial. That meant that any sort of factory could be built between those two railroads. In addition, the land was just off of N. J. Rt. 206 . . . a major North-South highway and was less than one half of a mile from an interchange of the new proposed Interstate 95. You did not need to be a rocket scientist to know that this was a very valuable piece of property.

I really did not know what to do, I did not have anyone to buy this property but I knew it was hot. My brother was on Vacation in Porto Rico so I called him ask who was capable of buying it. He gave me several names to call and I showed the land to each of them. The three different prospects that viewed the unlisted listing were all very interested to buy it.

Several days went by and Bob, my brother came back from vacation. I took him to see the property and he was just as enthused as I was. To make a long story short, I sold the property in less than ten days.

Sam Dresner, the owner said that he would pay a ten percent commission when the property closed. There was nothing in writing, he would not sign anything other than a contract to sell. It took several weeks or so to get the contracts, they were very extensive and over forty pages. When Sam did sign it he made sure that the commission was $54,000.

Two weeks later, I sold another piece of land in the same township for $350,000., the commission was $35,000. My share of these commissions was one half, just about $45,000.

The first deal closed about six months later and my share of the commission was $24,800. That was an astronomical amount of money for us and the second deal was closing in another month with a $17,000 commission. These two real estate deals were made during the six weeks of my recuperation.

Our business was making four or five hundred dollars a week and I truly thought that I had reached the pinnacle of business success.

Nevertheless I was constantly plagued by guilt if I did not attend a prayer meeting or frustration if I did. It was as if the prayer meeting pulled in one direction and what I wanted pulled in the other direction.

We had several local businessmen that attended these weekly gatherings. During one of the meetings Bob Jennings who owned the local "Ford" dealership suggested that I open our luncheonette on Friday nights for kids. It was to be a "Canteen" sort of thing to keep teenagers off the streets and to have a place to go. Fran Huber thought it was a great idea and so did all the others. I was "Horrified."

That was the last thing on earth that I wanted to do. We closed at 2:00 PM and that suited me fine. To be open at night and for teenagers was nothing but a nightmare for me. So I struggled with what I wanted and . . . "Is this what God wants ?"

After suffering with making this decision for two or three weeks I finally relented and decided to do it, very reluctantly at best. Arrangements were made to have extra help (all volunteers) and supplies. We advertised in the local paper and put up fliers up all over town.

Then the most startling thing occurred or my expertise at rationalization came into play, not sure which. We opened on Friday night from 5:00PM-11:00PM. The first Friday night NOT A SINGLE TEENAGER OR CUSTOMER CAME IN. We were all surprised at that and needless to say, I was delighted. I was ecstatic, no one knew that but I was. Joyce, my wife knew but no one else did.

That was enough for me to end it right then and there. Now being convinced that if God wanted me to do this, we would have had a store full of kids and we didn't so He must not want us to do this. I now had the perfect out. But it was only the first week and everyone thought that we should keep trying. I have always struggled with what God wanted me to do and with what I wanted to do, still do. I didn't want everyone to know that I did not want to do what God might want me to do so I faked it. We opened the following Friday and the same thing happened . . . no one came in the store. I was delighted and announced to the group that we would no longer be doing this anymore.

During the next few days Fran suggested to me that maybe God just wanted me to say yes to Him. That was music to my ears. I accepted that but must admit that deep down inside I was most fearful of more yes's to come. These sort of conflicts within myself really started to sour me on the prayer meetings. This kind of thing turned out to be short lived, with my newfound interest and success in real estate we decided to sell the business.

As the months went by going to church in Plainfield became a burden due to the time involved. (More than likely a handy rationalization of mine.) Between the travel time and the length of the service it almost took up an entire day. We would leave for church at 7:30 or 8:00 AM and not be back home until 2:30 or 3:00 o'clock in the afternoon.

In addition there were two or three prayer meetings during the week. It was beginning to feel like a battle between what I wanted and what God wanted. I had always just assumed that I could do as I pleased but now it was getting confusing and complicated. "I wanted to do this but did God want me to do that". These constant conflicts were keeping me from living my life the way I wanted. Real estate was also taking a significant amount of time, both due to playing and working.

Playing in the sense of stopping for a drink three or four times a week to play "Liar's Poker", going out to long lunches, playing golf, going to the track (race track), etc. I mean after all . . . I had arrived, I was entitled, heh . . . heh. Finally the first deal closed and the first thing that I did was to make arrangements for a ten day vacation to St Maarten in the Caribbean. The second thing that I did was to buy a Mercedes Benz, a magnificent 280 SEL. Did I go to church and thank God ? I'm ashamed to say that I honestly do not remember but I don't think so.

The playing that I referred to was actually a bit more than stopping for a drink now and then. There was a group of us that included several lawyers, several builders and several real estate people. There were three or four different watering holes that we used to frequent. One of which was the Clinton House. The Clinton House was an exclusive, very old and rustic inn that had been in existence for over two hundred years and it was a local gathering place. It had great steaks and had a very popular cocktail lounge.

One afternoon several of our group stopped for a drink. Most if not all of the group were older than me. I was twenty eight years of age. It was a rather unique group in that everyone truly excelled in their own area of expertise. In addition each of us were extremely successful financially and all of the personalities meshed almost like a completed puzzle. I wouldn't go so far as to say that we were a bunch of "Good old boys" but then again we were pretty close to it. We were well connected to local and state politicians, financial institutions etc. Doing business was exciting, stimulating and very profitable.

My brother Bob was 35 at the time. He was a straight laced disciplinarian and looked and acted like a Marine Corp. drill sergeant. Cal Sargent was fifty years old, very vain and virile. He was a very astute builder and real estate broker. He was fifty but wanted everyone to know that he was as good and strong as he was when he was twenty five. John Marucci was about forty five, Italian, dark hair, good looking, great sense of humor and was a builder.

Bob Benbrook was a lawyer and was a year older than me. He was a tall, lanky Irishman. Benbrook was the latter half of the law firm known as "Morrow and Benbrook". He had that look in his eye that Shakespeare recognized back in the fifteen hundreds. He had a rather unkept backwater look but was a very able and shrewd attorney. His partner on the other hand was polished well spoken and impeccably dressed. Morrow's office was elegantly furnished with oak desks and leather furniture. Benbrook's office had a haphazard disorganized look but it wasn't, he was sharp and knew where every file was located. It certainly was not a match made in heaven but it worked,

I was a very avid New York Jet and especially a Joe Namath fan. He unexpectedly won the super bowl several years prior. All of those that were in our group disliked Joe Namath and his flamboyant ways and I was always defending him. To make matters worse, he had had several bad and declining years on the football field and all of those guys were always razzing me about it. But in spite of that I was still a big fan.

My brother was friends with Richie Barre, he owned a local gentleman's farm. He also owned the very prosperous and popular company that made men's cologne called "Fabrage." They had an extensive advertising campaign utilizing famous athletes and personalities etc. When Richie Barre was negotiating with one of these stars he usually brought them out to his farm to do so.

One particular afternoon we stopped for a drink at the Clinton House. Most of the usual guys were there. Unbeknownst to any of us except my brother, Ritchie Barre was in the restaurant with Joe Namath. Joe Namath was one of my hero's along with Willie Mays and Muhammad Ali.

My brother went over to Richie and Joe to tell them how I felt about Joe and the Jets and how I was always defending them. I was sitting at a table with all the guys in the lounge. Out of the blue Joe Namath walks up to the table and asks for Tom . . . . I was dumbfounded. Joe shakes hands with me and tells the bartender to buy this table a drink. He then asks if I have any kids and signs autographs for all three of them. Talk about being on cloud nine, well there I sat smiling at the rest of this bunch. These sort of afternoons happened quite often.

All of these guys were doing well and we spent a lot of time together doing business and socially. We even got together with our wives. Benbrook just loved a Chinese restaurant locate up in the Pocono's. So we all went up there for dinner one Saturday night with our wives. After dinner we went to the Pocono Sheraton for a few drinks and dancing. My conservative brother had just purchased a 1974 Mercedes-Benz 450SEL. That was a very expensive new model. My brother liked to keep things like that quiet and always tried to be on the "Low key" side especially with the local townfolk. All the guys at the table knew about the car and also Bob's efforts to remain quiet and low key. The band was playing and we were dancing and drinking. The place was full and the music was loud. The band then played Janis Joplin's hit song "Daddy Won't You Buy Me a Mercedes-Benz." As my brother Bob was cowering the rest of the table roared in laughter. Business was good for all, it was fun and going to work was not even going to work.

On another occasion several of us went to the annual antique automobile show and flea market in Hershey, Pa. That was held the second week of October every year and was a gigantic gathering of antique car enthusiasts. As we strolled through the acres and acres of antique cars, I spotted a 1941 Chevy truck. It was painted bright red and looked like an armored truck. I loved the truck and bought it.

The ride home was about two hours long and during that ride my brother kept asking me what I was going to do with that truck. I did not know but he kept asking. Finally I got so sick of the question that I said; "How do I know, I'm going to paint "Chili, Chowder, Chicken-Parts and Prize Fights" on it." We laughed and we really laughed hard.

During slow days with no appointments I drove the truck to the office. My office was upstairs and one day several weeks later our secretary on the ground floor buzzed me. She said that there was a state inspector from the department of agriculture here to see me. I could not imagine what he would want and said to send him up. As he was climbing up the stairs I got up to meet him at the top of the staircase. He introduced himself and said that he was here to inspect the chickens. "Chickens, what chickens I said." He said "The ones advertised on your truck." You see when I got that truck back from Hershey, Pa. I had "Chili, Chowder, Chicken-Parts and Prizefights" gold leafed on both sides of the truck. I laughed and told the inspector the story and that there were no chickens to inspect. Fortunately, he laughed too. If ever there were glory days of real estate, it was then.

We had about twenty sales people in our office and all of them were doing well. Some would sell homes, some land for development and some specialized in commercial and industrial real estate. Our office was the premier real estate office in the county. We consistently sold large parcels of land involving large commissions. Each of these large deals enhanced our reputation.

It was decided to hire an evaluation firm to test all of our sales people to determine who should specialize in the various areas of real state. That turned out to be a comical and naïve experience regarding myself. I remember sitting at my interview with the evaluator and my brother. He asked me where I expected to be and doing in five years. I pondered the question, keep in mind that I had just closed on a million dollars of real estate deals. I answered him and said; "Gee, I'm not really sure." "I guess I'll be working several hours a day making deals, I'm happy doing what I'm doing now." As far as I was concerned I was in the perfect place at the perfect time. He laughed and looked at my brother. As they chuckled at each other, you could almost read their minds . . . "Is this guy for real?" However, in my mind I had arrived and my success was going to last indefinitely. Talk about naïve, I really believed that.

When all of the evaluations were completed the company provided suggestions as to what area each individual should be concentrating. The recommendations for me were to continue doing what I was doing and to get involved with sales management.

All of the guys in our group played golf. They used to go to the country club every Wednesday have lunch, play golf, have dinner and then play gin rummy until whenever. It sure sounded like a nice way to me to spend the day. So I joined the country club, bought a set of "Ping" golf clubs, "Foot Joy" golf shoes and a leopard skin golf bag and was all set to play golf with the boys.

The first Wednesday I drove up to the club, the guys were already there having lunch. They came out to help me unload the clubs, etc. I opened the trunk to my Mercedes, they took one look at my new toys and all started laughing.

I thought all of that good stuff was going to make me a scratch golfer . . . Ha . . . they knew better and they were right. Arrangements were made at the club for golf lessons and for the next month or so I played golf every Wednesday. However, the lessons did not help I did not improve and did not like golf. But I did like the lunches and the gin rummy.

I think that I avoided God and church because I did not want that to interfere with my newfound wealth and what I wanted to do. If I went to church I might have to do what God wanted me to do. If there was a football game on and a prayer meeting at the same time . . . . Frustration if I went to the prayer meeting . . . . Guilt if I went to the football game.

It became simpler if we just went back to the Catholic church. That would not take so much time, there would not be that confusion or that frustration, etc. It was also a quick and easy answer to my feelings of guilt, feelings that I hated. That is what we did and in a relatively short period of time I was back to dropping Joyce and the kids off and picking them up on Sunday.

CHAPTER 3

More bumps in the road

There is an indefinable mysterious power that pervades everything. I feel it, though I do not see it. It is this unseen power that makes itself felt and yet defies proof, because it is so unlike all that I perceive . . . . Gandhi

Several years passed by and a number of things had occurred that seriously adversely affected the real estate business. Mortgage money became extremely hard to come by and there was now a very severe gasoline shortage. These circumstances basically created a depression in the real estate and development business. Coupled with the playing and lack of preparation for times like this, we found ourselves with serious financial difficulty.

I had to leave the real estate business due to the commission basis of getting paid. Oftentimes it took months from start to finish to get paid. That no longer worked for us.

Then two incredible events occurred. The first was: We had a tradition in our family, when one of us had a birthday that person could have whatever they wanted for their birthday dinner. It was my oldest daughter Patty's birthday . . . November 15th and she wanted an Italian sub sandwich for her dinner. We were in dire straits and I did not have any money. My wife had been baking bread so that was not a problem. I scrounged up a dollar or two to get a half of a pound of salami. Then the most miraculous thing happened. It was mid November and we had already had several hard frosts.

We had a large fenced in garden and Joyce said that she was going to go to see if she could find some vegetables. I laughed and said "it would be a waste of time, it had already frozen out there several times". She went anyway and came back with two large perfect tomatoes and a good size onion. Just the things one would need to make Italian sub sandwiches.

I was shocked and couldn't believe it . . . she was not and thanked God. I must say that it did make me wonder . . . and I really did wonder. We were truly that broke and yes, God did provide for my daughter's birthday.

The second occurrence was: I had no job and no income and went to a "Head Hunting" agency in New York City. They secured an interview with a large real estate developer that was located in Cleveland, Ohio. They were looking for a sales manager. The interview went very well I thought and they said they would be in touch in a few days. The very next day they called me to say that I was not qualified for the job. However, they did have a sales opening and they wanted me to come to Cleveland for another interview and they would send me a plane ticket. I reluctantly said OK. I did not want a commission sales job.

The next day the ticket arrived via Federal Express, it was for the following day. I was to take off from Newark at 3:00 o'clock in the afternoon, arrive in Cleveland at 6:00 o'clock, have the interview and return to Newark departing Cleveland at 11 0'clock that same night.

I did not want that job and I was not going to go. Joyce pleaded with me to go. She said she had been praying for a long time and that they were going to offer me a different job, a much better job. I resisted and she insisted so I went for the interview just to please her.

When I arrived in Cleveland I was picked up and driven to the headquarters of Forest City Enterprises. There were six or seven other candidates for two available jobs. The interview was going to be a "Round Robin" circumstance. There were three different men that had to interview each of us and each session would be timed. The decision would be made tonight.

When we completed the interviews we were either asked to wait in the lobby or dismissed. After my interviews I was asked to wait in the lobby. There was one other candidate waiting as well. His name was Neal Lader . . . . and to this day he is still a very dear and valued friend, twenty seven years hence.

One of the interviewers came into the lobby and said . . . . there was going to be a change and that they wanted me to talk to the executive vice president. Needless to say, I was bewildered and was escorted into his office. When I sat down he said "WE WOULD LIKE TO OFFER YOU A DIFFERENT POSITION THAN WHAT YOU CAME FOR. OUR CLEVELAND AREA IS DIVIDED INTO FOUR SECTIONS AND EACH HAS A PROJECT MANAGER, WE WANT YOU TO BE A PROJECT MANAGER". He went on to describe the position, the salary, expenses, etc . . . . No commissions.

Well you talk about shock, all I could think of was Joyce pleading for me to go because I was going to come home with a much better job. Sure enough, she was right and I accepted the job.

My flight home that night was nothing short of euphoric, I just could not believe it. Joyce was right, I was coming home with a different job than what I thought. I sat on that plane thinking about Joyce and all of her prayers. Could it be God answering her prayers or was it just the way things happen. I was plagued with doubts about God.

When I arrived home at about 2:30 AM Joyce was up and waiting for me. There were no cell phones in those days so she did not know. Strangely enough when I opened the front door she did know. She really did know and was overjoyed.

We moved to Cleveland at the new company's expense and shortly thereafter started the new job. The other fellow in the Company lobby that night was also hired as a project manager, his name was Neal Lader.

Forest City Enterprises was a number of companies that were all involved in various disciplines of real estate development. Our particular division had to do with getting the approvals of various residential projects and building and installing the improvements required, roads, water mains, sewers, etc.

The company paid for the move and all other expenses. The transition was smooth and we joined the Catholic church in our new location Chagrin Falls, Ohio.

Joyce and the kids went to church every Sunday. I still only dropped them off and picked them up. She also was involved in several prayer groups and really loved the church. She wanted me to join her at those prayer meetings but I did want to return to confusion that I experienced at the Plainfield, N. J. meetings.

The job as great and things were fine for about six months. Then there was a company meeting and they announced that there was going to be a slow down and a number of projects were going to be stopped. One week later there was another meeting and sure enough they stopped most of the projects and laid off several of the project managers. However, I was not one of them.

The prime interest rate had risen to nineteen percent. That made it impossible for any real estate project to proceed. The company kept several of the project managers to administer the holdings, pay the taxes, etc. and I was one of them. I was a survivor.

However, three months later there was another lay off and this time I too was laid off. The prime interest rate was now over twenty percent. A lethal circumstance in the real estate business. The company gave me six months pay and said that they would move us anywhere in the country that we wanted to move.

That is when we decided to move to Cape Cod. We had been through the mill in New Jersey and just didn't want to go back there. We always loved the ocean and spent a lot of time there. So we decided to go to Cape Cod to be near the water.

I fully expected to get a position with a commercial real estate developer in or around Boston. However, after we arrived there we found the same real estate depression that we left in Cleveland. I spent the better part of the next six months commuting to Boston several times a week searching for work, to no avail.

CHAPTER 4

A new beginning

My Lord God, I have no idea where I am going. I do not see the road a head of me. I cannot know for certain where it will end. Nor do I really know myself, and the fact that I think that I am following your will does not mean that I am actually doing so. But I believe that the desire to please you does in fact please you. And I hope that I have that desire in all that I am doing. I hope that I will never do anything apart from that desire. And I know that if I do this you will lead me by the right road though I may know nothing about it. Therefore I will trust you always though I may seem to be lost and in the shadow of death. I will not fear, for you are ever with me, and you will never leave me to face my perils alone.

THOMAS MERTON

Our son was working at a deli up the street from where we lived and it was for sale. It was a very similar business to the one that we owned in Flemington, N. J. It was a breakfast and lunch place and very busy especially in the summer. I was interested but not that interested because I did not have enough money to buy it. Once again my wife pushed me to go talk to the owner . . . she was still going to church and praying everyday.

I went to see the owner and coincidentally they were also from N. J. We had a lot in common and hit it off very well. He had moved up here with his whole family to run this business and they all hated it. Busy as it was, it was being run as a greasy spoon and was severely neglected due to the fact that they all wanted to sell and move back o N. J. They wanted one hundred and ten thousand dollars for the business and real estate.

My oldest brother (the Marine type) and my Father came up from N. J. to take a look at the business and give me some advice. My brother did not know anything about the business but he did know about real estate. My Father had spent most of his life in the restaurant business and thought that it was a dream situation. He loved the hours of operation 6:00 AM-2:00 PM and the numbers were good.

My Father and brother actually negotiated the deal. We bought the place with no money down for ninety thousand dollars. We had a first mortgage from the bank for $70,000. and a second mortgage for $20,000. from the owner payable over the next five years. We opened for business on February 23, 1981.

The place needed a lot of clean up because it had been uncared for so long. This was a seven day a week business and the first week or so I laid in bed at night asking myself . . . oh God what have I done? Everything settled down, we changed a few things and business really prospered.

The seven days a week was a problem but with the mortgages that had to be paid there really wasn't any choice. I had also borrowed an additional ten thousand dollars for start up money.

Joyce and the kids were going to the local Catholic church but had to stop due to the seven days a week. Our youngest daughter continued to be dropped off every Sunday for First Holy Communion classes. She and Joyce went to church on Sundays during that time but no one else did. Business really thrived and we paid off all of the loans except the first mortgage in two years.

During the months of May thru September most of our customers were college kids working and living on Cape Cod for the summer. Serving breakfast was about seventy per cent of our volume. We used about fifteen cases of eggs each case containing thirty dozen eggs. a week. That's a lotta eggs for a twenty eight seat restaurant. The summertime was so busy we had a line out the door and down the street.

The focus of our business changed after Labor Day to lunch for local business people. We still served breakfast but not to the extent that we did in the summer. Business continued to improve and we developed a Cape wide reputation for being one of the best places to eat on Cape Cod. Then in 1984 we experienced a major complication, I was diagnosed with multiple sclerosis.

The best place for me to begin is the day I was diagnosed. I was on my way to the gym, to work out. When I got out of my car, I had the most horrific sensations around my waist. I felt like a frozen Milky Way and I was about to crack in half. It was an incredible struggle to maintain my balance, and to walk. I managed to get inside to the gym but I felt so strange that I decided to go home. It was quite a struggle to get back to the car. When I arrived home I called the Lahey Clinic in Boston and told them what happened. They made an appointment for me for the next day.

I had spinal surgery on my neck in 1970 and again in 1971 and I thought this was the problem. I gathered up my x-rays and went to the doctor the next day. It was a Friday and my appointment was late afternoon with a neurosurgeon. I explained about the neck surgeries that were done in the early seventies. He said he wanted to do a mylegram to see if there was a blockage. I did not understand what he meant by a blockage, but I knew I was in trouble. You just don't do an unscheduled mylegram late on a Friday afternoon.

After the mylegram was done he came in to tell me there was no brain tumor. I was then glad that I did not know what he meant by a blockage. That would have scared me to death. He turned me over to a neurologist. It was extremely fortunate for me to be turned over to this particular neurologist. She became my primary MS doctor and had been most supportive, realistic, empathetic and respectful of my thoughts until her recent retirement. She has been very instrumental and responsible for my success with this marathon, MS.

My doctor wanted me to tell her of my earliest symptoms, when, where, and what they were, in detail. I began by telling of some strange feelings that I was having as early as 1964. From time to time it felt like I was walking on marbles. There were times when it was unusual swallowing. This is a symptom that has never returned to this day. If I reached in my pocket for a dime, I would have to take everything out of that pocket and look at it to get the dime. For years, it felt as though I had an ace bandage wrapped around my waist; it still does. These things would come and go. I would go to a doctor, he would not know what it was and send me to another doctor. This went on for several years. I stopped going to doctors because none of them could ever find anything wrong. Several more years went by relatively symptom free, and then they started to come back.

I went to a doctor in New York City that was recommended by a doctor that my father knew. After he examined me and I explained my history, he said I had a virus and to go home and don't worry about it, just live your life. Well that was exactly what I wanted to hear and that is just what I did. I was 22 years of age and it sounded good to me. This was the first time a doctor said this to me and he was right. When he said that I had a virus he never mentioned MS. That was the best thing that he could have done for me.

A year or so later I was buying a life insurance policy and was turned down. The doctor in NYC had reported that I had MS. Needless to say, I was shocked and dismayed.

My brother lived next to a doctor who knew a neurosurgeon that was said to be one of the best in the country and he said that I should go to him. That is what I did and he said that I did not have MS. He said that I had a nerve in my neck that was being encroached by a deteriorating disc. There was a serious danger of the nerve being severely and permanently damaged. He said that he could solve the problem by removing the damaged disc and replacing it with a piece of bone from my hip and fusing the vertebrae in my neck. He did the cervical lamenectomy to eliminate the problem.

Several months later I still had all the same symptoms and he suggested another operation. I did not get a second opinion and was so tired of going to doctors, this doctor was supposed to the best so why bother? He did the second operation, removing the rear portions of bone on the vertebrae in my neck. The operation was supposed to relieve some pressure on my spinal cord and eliminate the problems that I was having. Several months went by and all the symptoms came back again, I'm not even sure that they ever left. This operation did not work either so I just stopped going to doctors and decided to live with it.

I guess that I got used to it and it was not so bad and did not stop me from doing anything. The good thing was that I proved to the life insurance company that I did not have MS and I got the life insurance.

A year or two passed when I received an announcement in the mail that the neurosurgeon was retiring. The announcement stated that he had arthritis in his hands and could no longer operate. It also stated that my records were being sent to another surgeon and that I should register as a new patient with that doctor. I did that and they asked me to come in for a routine neurological exam. During that exam this new doctor also said that I did not have MS.

When I got to this part of the story as the doctor was taking down my history, she said, the doctor in New York was right; you have a virus and the virus is MS. It was incredible when she said that. I instantly felt my mind switch gears and get set to defend itself. It was as though I just experienced the worst betrayal of my life. I felt panic and horror and disbelief all at the same time.

I spent the next half-hour trying to prove to her that I did not have MS. I was in total denial and frantic; in my mind this was impossible. I was trying to convince Dr Lessell that she made a horrible mistake and I could prove it . . . I got the life insurance. I kept repeating over and over that they never would have given me the life insurance if I had MS. There were also two prominent neurosurgeons that assured me that I did not have MS. I felt like a fish that just took the bait, and was wriggling to get off the hook. Well needless to say, I did not get off the hook.

It was now about 9:00 P. M. They called my wife and told her that I had a problem and she would have to come and pick me up. They would not tell her on the phone what the problem was. By the time she arrived, it was about 11:30 P. M. While I was waiting Dr. Lessell tried to soothe me and explain a number of things about MS. She said that due to the mylegram I might have difficulty urinating. If I did, go to the local hospital, tell them I was just diagnosed with MS and they would catherize me. Catherize me! I was shocked that this could be happening to me . . . . as soon as tonight. It felt as though this whole circumstance was a bad dream, a nightmare would be more like it. She also said that I might have difficulty walking for the next few days because of the mylegram. It was hard to comprehend what was happening. Several hours ago, I walked into this clinic and now I was talking about getting catheterized and was not able to walk.

By this time, I was out of bed, sitting in a wheelchair waiting for my wife. As we continued talking all kinds of thoughts were racing through my head. Questions, answers, what ifs, etc. My mind was going so fast it was impossible to keep up with it. I asked, what happens next? She said just go home and let this sink in. Talk to your wife. Call me at anytime for any questions. Remember that you are thinking the worst; you are thinking of the posters that you have seen about MS. They are always the most terrible cases so they get attention, and raise funds. Go home, call me tomorrow morning and I'll see you next week.

I was not panic stricken but that is as close to it as I have ever been, before or since. I remember rambling about owning a deli with my family, saying that we all work there. My wife, my oldest daughter is 22 and my oldest son is 20. They are very capable, they can do it. They were almost panic thoughts. I knew that I was actually trying to convince myself that everything was going to work out but I also knew that I did not believe my own words. My youngest son is mildly retarded and 19. My youngest daughter is only 7. How do I tell them about this? She said, "there are a lot of things running through your head after a few days everything will settle down and you will begin to get some answers". I did not like her response. In fact, I hated it, and I wanted a solution right now. She was right; after several days everything did begin to settle down.

When they wheeled me to the car, I could not pick up my feet. I could stand but I had no balance and my legs felt like stilts. There was no feeling in my feet. I got into the car and we started the drive home. I remember saying to Joyce, this is like something you see in the movies and this is the end of the movie. At that moment, I really thought my life was over. Our lives were over. I always considered our love remarkable; we were best friends and now it was over. I just couldn't believe it. All the way home I had those damn questions and what ifs. Fortunately, I am a talker.

In high school, I was voted the most talkative. All the way home we talked. Each time I brought up one of my worries, Joyce said, stop worrying we'll cross that bridge when we come to it. I was usually the one to say that but not this time. When we got home it was well after midnight. I struggled to get out of the car and into the house. I had to constantly hold on to something and I felt like I was going to crack in half at the waist. I do not remember much else about that night but I remember the night, the MS night.

Our deli deli opened at 5:30 A. M. While we were at the hospital I called my Father who lived in N. J. to tell him the news and ask him to come and help us. The next morning everyone except me got up early and went to work.

About 7 o'clock I struggled to the car and got to the deli. The deli was only a block and a half away. I don't remember much about how I drove the car but I did. What I vividly remember is sitting at a table where I always had coffee. A lot of customers would come and sit with me every morning and we would talk about anything and everything. This particular morning was different from any other. As different people would talk, I either had no interest in what they were saying or I didn't even hear them. These people were friends that I had been having coffee with for years. No one knew that I was just diagnosed with MS and I did not know how or if I should tell him or her. My mind was racing and I just could not cope with sitting there. It was impossible to concentrate on anything. I left and started to go home. It took me about thirty minutes to get up from the table, go to the back door, down two steps to the car. The car was parked about ten feet from those steps and I could not get to the car. Someone had to help me. I burst into tears. Never in my life had I ever felt such gloom. I think someone drove me home but I don't remember.

I called Dr. Less ell, it was about 9:00 A. M. I was scared stiff, my mind was racing with fears and questions. I asked her what I could expect and what was going to happen next? She answered with a number of best and worst case scenarios. I could not get the worst-case scenarios out of my mind. I asked her when I would have to be catheterized. She laughed and said, "that may never happen, stop thinking the worst". I remember thinking, how can she be laughing, this is the worst. Then she said something that I passed over very lightly at the time. What she said as it turns out, became the most helpful and important medicine that I ever could have asked for? She said, "The best predictor of the future of this disease is to look at your past and your past is good." You have had MS for a long time, your symptoms go back many years and you have done very well. That statement did not mean much to me at the time. However, I'm still doing reasonably well and that statement is one of the reasons. Years later, whenever I experienced a new sensation or potential problem, rather than think I was getting worse, I thought of my past, and my past was good. That one single statement has proven to be a major building block for motivation.

There were so many questions in that conversation and none of the answers were answers that I wanted. Finally she said, "This is going to be an ongoing learning process". You are coming in for several more tests next week; we will discuss it then. We hung up the phone and I sat in my kitchen in disbelief. My father and brother arrived a short time later. We sat and talked for most of the day about my options. I could not concentrate or stay focused on anything we discussed. My mind kept racing and asking itself, how could this be? I was unable to walk without holding on to cabinets or walls or anything else that was fixed. About 4:30 P. M. I went into the bedroom to lie down. I was incredibly depressed, so was everyone else. My seven-year-old, a very active extrovert came to the bed and asked what was wrong daddy? She was always so full of life and had an admirable independent spirit. I did not know how to answer her. She walked away shrugging her shoulders and very solemn. At that moment, I remember thinking "If you don't snap out of this, you're going to destroy this whole family". How do I snap out of it? No answer. I hated that feeling of not having an answer. I was not accustomed to having a problem that did not have an answer. I got up and went into the kitchen. We all had dinner and I do not remember much about the rest of the evening. What sticks out in my mind is the difficulty that I had staying with a conversation. This was the same thing that happened to me earlier that day at the deli. As everyone talked, I was wondering how they could be talking about such trivial matters. In my mind, I did not have answers about anything to do with MS and nothing else seemed to matter. Several times I had to go to the bathroom. I still had that feeling like I was going to crack in half at the waist. It was as if I was paralyzed from the waist down. It is hard to explain because I could feel everything but it was so difficult to move my feet and legs. It was such a battle each time that I went to the bathroom; I ultimately got depressed and went to bed.

As I lay there I could not figure out how I was going to get out of this. My youngest daughter Jennifer was a very precocious seven-year-old. She was totally unwilling to accept this uncharacteristic behavior she now saw in me. She was very serious when she said, "daddy, I know you can do it, I know you can walk". You have to try harder. I said OK and struggled back to the table. Later that night after we all went to bed, there is no doubt in my mind that a genuine miracle occurred. I was born and raised Catholic but had not been practicing my faith. Even though I had not been an active Church go'er, I had a strong belief in God. I could not understand why he let or made this happen. I considered myself a good person, a faithful husband, and a decent father. I did not deserve or have time for multiple sclerosis. So how can this be?

About two o'clock in the morning, I woke up. I struggled to get into the kitchen and sat at the kitchen table. There I was sitting at my table smoking a cigarette. I heard this voice. It said: "You don't deserve MS and you don't have time for MS but you have it. What you really don't have time for, is to sulk about it. There will be a way to overcome it, there are reasons for this, have faith. Consider your wife, consider your children, you all have things to learn and experience. Have faith; I will not forsake you." I could not believe it, for a moment I thought I might be going mad. Did I really hear this or was it wishful thinking? Yes, I heard those words they were unmistakable.

All of a sudden there was no depression, no self-pity, no worry and most of all, no fear. It was as if a light switch had been turned on. One-minute deep dark depression, the next bright lights and optimism, it was that fast. It was now about 4:00 A. M. and the family was starting to get up. I was very excited with my newly found good spirits. Needless to say, the rest of the family was thrilled, to say the least.

In May our deli was very busy on weekends and today was Sunday. The deli was only a block down the street and everyone went to work. My father and brother stayed at a motel so I was home alone with Jennifer. I was able to walk with a little less difficulty. I still had to hold on to something but I no longer felt like I was going to crack in half. I was able to get to the car and drive to the deli. I should not have done that because my feet were moving very sluggishly but I could move them and that was exciting. I cannot tell you how I managed to drive. It was only one block but I still should not have done that.

When I arrived at the deli everyone was happy, excited and concerned all at the same time. I told them what had happened during the night. It was extraordinary how my change of attitude instantly changed everyone else's as well. I am convinced that God brought me out of that abyss of doom and depression. For about thirty hours I felt doom that I have never, never experienced before. I could not have brought myself out of that state alone. God was right there with me, His Grace did it.

I continued to improve both mentally and physically as the day progressed. You might say this was my first real lesson in communication. As I continued to improve, I was also remembering some of the things Dr. Lessell said to me Friday night. She said that because of the mylegram I might have difficulty walking for a few days. I did not remember that until my walking began to come back. Apparently when she said that, I was in such a state that I didn't listen. I had no recollection of her saying that until my walking improved. When I realized this, I wondered what else I might have missed or what other false conclusions I might have come to. I did remember her comment about the past being the best predictor of the future with this disease. I did remember her saying that my past was good and that I have done well with this. This recollection made me very positive and enthusiastic.

That Sunday afternoon, Joyce and I drove up to the beach to talk. It was the first time we were alone since Friday night when this entire trauma began. It felt good to be by ourselves; we had a lot to talk about. Dr Lessell mentioned that my eyesight might be affected by this MS problem. That really scared me and I was also in a panic about our sex lives. The potential loss of those two things was a fate worse than death. Joyce said, you are not having any eye problems now and tonight lets make love. She had this incredible attitude that gave me great comfort and removed most of my fears. The two things that I was most concerned about didn't even faze her. I began to feel safe and open. She said, this is a nerve disease not a muscle disease; you can still keep your muscles strong. That was a startling revelation. I never thought of that. I had a full-blown gym in my basement and had been working out everyday for several years. I thought those days were going to be over now, Joyce's comment was like an awakening. The workouts would continue. I was extremely encouraged and excited. The more we talked, the more relaxed, peaceful and excited we both became. The apprehension that this diagnosis created began to dissipate. We were at the beach for about two hours talking. Before we left we agreed that it was absolutely critical that we spend an hour or so alone just to talk, every day. We have been faithful to that agreement to this day and it has enhanced every facet of our lives.

A week or so after my initial diagnosis I returned to Dr Lessell for several tests, brain scan, reaction tests etc. I did not see Dr. Lessell for long because of these tests that were being done. I was to return in about a month to determine a course of action. The one thing that she did emphatically say to me was to go home and live my life, don't worry. This was the second time that a doctor told me to just go home and live my life. The first time was in 1970, by the doctor in New York.

Each day I continued to improve and within a week or so things were just about back to normal. MS is a very mysterious and erratic circumstance. Symptoms and come and go in the blink of an eye and then again they can remain for an extended period of time. I was relatively symptom free for several years and continued on with my life as it had been before being diagnosed.

However, we had some new and different family problems which in turn made some difficult business problems. It was 1991 and my son unexpectedly left the deli. The plan had always been for him to take over the business. We had a neighbor that lived two doors down the street from us and she was looking for a job. At that time we did not know her very well but we were really in a jam and needed someone to replace my son right away. Her first day of work was the first indication of her outstanding character.

It had been snowing for a day and a half and there was twenty four inches of snow on the ground. We were still open because the deli was the local gathering place for most of the local folks and most of the drivers of the snow plows would be in and out of the deli.

Well with all that snow the roads were close to impassable and in trudges Peggy Hollum, my new employee. She walked to work ! I laughed and thanked the good Lord at the same time. Who would ever have thought that anyone especially a new employee would come to work on a day like today? That was the start of a long relationship that would shift from being an employee-employer relationship to being a very valued and loyal friend. She stood by us through an awful lot of troubles.

We operated the deli for another five years, however, we had to make some changes to lighten the burden that was on Joyce. These changes cost us a significant amount of business and after several years things got pretty rough financially.

That is when we stated thinking about selling the deli. The deli was next door to a church thrift shop. One afternoon a woman lost control of her car and hit the side if the thrift shop building. When she did that she also knocked the natural gas meter off the outside wall. It was after closing and my wife had gone to the bank. Someone called the fire company and they came to evacuate the three contiguous buildings. I was not able to walk and was sitting in the dining room in one of our restaurant chairs. Peggy and two firemen picked me up in the chair and carried me out of the building sitting in the chair. They set me down in the street several hundred feet away. Fire trucks were blocking both ends of the street and there I sat in the middle of them.

I remember thinking; "Geez, with a little luck the deli will burn down . . . that will solve our financial problems". No such luck. As this was going on Joyce came back from the bank but could not get through to the deli with the car. So she comes running up to Peggy and I in the street in a panic not knowing what has happened. By this time the firemen had shut off the gas and the danger was no longer . . . . My thoughts, only to myself; "Shucks, almost". These new troubles coupled with the ms that we were experiencing put a much greater burden on Joyce. So in June of 1996 we sold the deli.

CHAPTER 5

Miracles DO happen

Do not be afraid, for I have redeemed you;
I have called you by your name, you are mine.
Should you pass through the sea, I will be with you;
Or through rivers, they will not swallow you up.
Should you walk through fire, you will not be scorched
And the flames will not burn you.
For I am Yahweh, your God,
The holy one of Israel, your saviour.

ISAIAH 43:2-3

After the transfer of the business and real estate closing we were left with approximately $120.000. I invested $90,000. in four stocks. The stock symbols were ATIS, MUCP, MOOR and CITN. They traded on the over-the-counter market and each were valued between two and four dollars a share. I was attempting to make a killing in the market, my goals at the time were still to make as much money as I could. We had a capitol gain tax of $37,000. to pay. However, it was June and that tax did not have to be paid until the following April so I decided to wait until then to pay it. Little did I know what was to come.

Several months passed by and both Joyce and I were somewhat bored and we started looking for a business that was less demanding. In October of 1996 we found a small Café' just about five miles away in Harwichport, Ma. We met with the owner and verbally agreed to terms and agreed to contact our respective attorneys to have contracts prepared. I wanted to do this but was quite uncertain if we should go through with the deal due to our limited funds. The stocks that I bought were not doing well and that is where the bulk of our money was.

My attorney was advised of the particulars and we proceeded to acquire all the necessary permits and licenses. Strangely enough no one was pressing to get the contracts signed. That suited me fine because as long as there was no signed contract, we could back out of the deal. The weeks went by and the next thing you know it was the middle of January. The deal was supposed to close on or about February 1, 1997.

We still had no signed contract and were still not sure if we should proceed. But soon we would have to make a decision. A date was made to sign contracts and we had a week to decide. No one involved knew that we were still not sure if we were going to go through with the deal. We decided to go sit in the parking lot and watch the Café" to observe the number of customers that went into the business daily. We sat there every day from 7:00AM-1:30 or 2:00PM.

Time was surely getting short we had two more days before we had to sign those contracts and come up with the deposit called for in the contract. The day before the last day we were sitting in the parking lot and it was drizzling and cloudy. At about 10:00AM the sun came out and it started to clear. I looked out of the window of the car and there was a magnificent full rainbow that spanned the entire sky. I was surprised and excited and turned to Joyce to tell her to look out the window. She was already looking out the window and had tears in her eyes. She knew about me and rainbows and said; "We can sign the contracts."

This was an extremely emotional and moving moment for us. Both of us were sure that were getting Divine guidance. We contacted our lawyer, signed the contracts and the closing was set for the next week.

The Cafe' had been primarily an ice cream parlor during the day and a take out pizza place at night. We were going to change it to a breakfast and lunch Café'. That involved removing the pizza ovens, redesigning the kitchen to make it handicapped accessible and workable for me. I was only able to stand for short periods of time and designed the kitchen to enable me to prep and cook in a draftsman's chair. This was a chair that would swivel back and forth and was on wheels. The prep tables were on my left and the stoves and ovens on my right.

We completed the renovations and redecorating and were set to open on February 23, 1997. Exactly sixteen years to the day after we opened the first deli. The night before the opening my brother in New Jersey called to tell me that our Father died during the night. Devastating news to say the least. Not so much that it was unexpected, he had been ailing for some time it is just one of those things that cannot be prepared for. Obviously we put off the opening and drove to New Jersey to attend my Dad's funeral. He was a one in a million Dad and would be sorely missed.

We returned to open the Café' and flourished. Harwichport is a small, quaint former Cape Cod fishing village that anxiously anticipated our opening. And flourish we did. We needed some help to run the Cafe', I called a woman that worked for us at the deli. Peggy Hollum, she was also a neighbor and friend. She lived two doors down from us and I hired her in 1991. At that time we barely knew each other but through the years we became much more than employee-employer. Not only did she become the most dedicated employee that we ever had, she also became a dedicated friend, possibly the best friend that I have ever had.

We implemented a limited breakfast menu that was not as intense or demanding as the menu at the deli. We also had several hot meals served at lunch everyday and closed at 2:00 PM. We were closed on Sundays and most holidays, something we had not done at the deli.

Nine and a half years ago, I went to confession for the first time in thirty-six years! I had not been in all those years because I did not think that it was necessary, I thought that I could just confess privately with God. My wife has a friend that is a very devout Catholic. Her name is Therese. Whenever she talks about God or Church she has the most unusual demeanor. There is an inner peace and joy that is so quiet and gentle that it compels you to be interested, very interested in what she has to say. One day she was talking about confession and in her usual manner, she suggested that I go. I smiled and didn't think much about it. However, for the next several days our conversation was constantly on my mind. Therese mentioned a particular priest that was visiting a local parish for a week. She said that he was hearing confessions all through the week and that anyone could call for an appointment to make their confession. I laughed, I had not been to confession since I got married thirty-six years ago and that was the last thing on my mind.

She smiled with her usual peace and that was the end of it. The next day I was alone in the kitchen cooking and for a split second the thought of going to confession crossed my mind. It was only for a second or two and for another second or two I wondered why I had that thought. The next morning again I was alone in the kitchen cooking. Once again I started thinking about going to confession. This time I was really puzzled and wondering why I was thinking of this again. At that same moment Therese walked into the kitchen. I quickly said, Therese maybe I'll go to confession. With that same smile she said, oh good here I have his phone number. I called the priest and made an appointment for the next day at 3:00 P. M. The priest's name was Father Vincent Youngberg, from Pelham, N.Y.

The last time that I had been to confession was when we were married, thirty-six years ago. At that time you went into a dark dingy booth with a curtain separating you from the priest so you didn't see each other. This time it was sitting face to face in a small library adjacent to the main church. The room was separated from the main church with a glass wall. My wife was waiting for me in the main church and we could see her through the glass wall. We sat and talked about my life and his life for about an hour and a half or so.

When my confession was finished, Father Youngberg gave me absolution. He then leaned forward and was staring right into my eyes. Our faces were only six inches apart. I felt like he was looking right into my brain. As he began to speak he was gesturing through the glass towards my wife. As he was doing this he said something to me that was absolutely astounding. In an instant I completely understood, as much as I am capable of understanding, God's love. He said, "God has been trying to show you His love through your wife." He was standing and pointing through the glass to my wife. That statement startled me and was like an instantaneous illumination. I could totally relate to and comprehend that love. I knew my wife Joyce's love for me and to think that God was showing me His love by that love, literally brought me to tears. That one profound statement has completely altered and changed every single value and the course of my life.

The very next day one of the lunchtime customers in our café came into the kitchen to show something to me. This was most unusual; he was a local lawyer and we were not friends. He reached into his pocket for a small leather zippered pouch. He said that this was given to him by the pastor of the local Catholic Church, Holy Trinity. It was a small glass case with Latin writings, within the case was a tiny splinter of wood. The splinter of wood had somehow been authenticated by the Catholic Church in Rome; to be a splinter of the original cross that Jesus Christ had been crucified on. My mind was puzzled and filled with questions. Why had this man come into my kitchen today? How can this splinter be from the original cross? What if it is from the original cross? All of these questions and thoughts were occurring simultaneously. Our minds are a miracle because when you ask it a question, it always answers. The answers came as quickly as the questions. Was God was trying to reach me? Could this be? Who knows? I sure did not know. First my confession to Father Vincent and his comment about God showing me His love. Then this splinter, if in fact this splinter was from the original cross, then I was holding in my hand, the blood of Jesus Christ! The one and only Jesus Christ. Just the thought of this possibility literally sent shivers through my entire body. This man could see that I was visibly moved He said, "You can keep it for a day or two, I was afraid to borrow it but I really wanted to and did.

My mind was racing with questions and I was extremely uncomfortable with the answers that I was getting. What's going on? What's happening here? That afternoon my wife and her friend asked me if I would like to go to benediction at church. I said no, "Its Tuesday not Sunday." I would not like to go and I was annoyed that they asked. I did not like religious fanatics and I was starting to feel like one. I went to the benediction at 4:00 P.M. that day, a Tuesday. When we arrived, I got out of the car and into my wheelchair. I did not like my wheelchair and this was the first time that I was going to church using it. At that time, it was not a practice of mine to attend church regularly. All of these circumstances made me feel very uncomfortable.

Unbeknownst to me, Therese went to the priest to tell him about the artifact that I was carrying. We were still outside, the little Polish priest came over, whom I had never met and asked to see it. He blessed it and himself and me. There were lots of people mulling around waiting to go into church. It was so uncomfortable for me that I felt as if I was going to jump out of my skin. The nagging questions. What am I doing here? What is happening? When the priest blessed me my eyes swelled up with tears. Is this emotionalism? If not, what is it? MS is always in the back of my mind so I assumed that my emotions had something to do with MS. Whatever, I had to let go because I could not come up with an answer that satisfied me.

We all finally went into church for benediction. This church has a chapel with perpetual adoration of the Blessed Sacrament that is where the benediction is held. This might have been the first time that I had ever been to benediction; I am not sure. For those of you that are not Catholic, The Blessed Sacrament is the living body of Christ. That is a mystery that we will never fully understand. But Jesus Christ Himself said; "This is My Body, this is My Blood, do this in remembrance of Me" at The Last Supper. Keep in mind that for fifteen hundred years after Christ's death there was only one Christian religion . . . Catholic. Benediction is the formal adoration of the body of Christ and the blessing of the congregation with the body of Christ by the priest or deacon.

This was quite a struggle for me to get through. Try as I might to believe in God and to understand benediction and the Blessed Sacrament, I had so many nagging doubts and questions. Interestingly enough, during benediction a most calming peace came over me. There were about twenty or thirty people in the chapel. They all sang and prayed as I wondered; is this really true? As I sat there listening and observing my eyes filled up with tears again. They just came, I couldn't stop them. My thoughts just produced more questions without answers. The benediction lasted about twenty minutes. When we left my wife and Therese were happy and giddy and I was incredibly perplexed. The next day there was a strong urge to return to the chapel and I did. I had also returned to going to Mass on Sundays.

It was the latter part of May and I continued to go to the chapel almost daily. The weeks seemed to fly by and it was now the fourth of July. We invited a few friends and they invited a few of their friends to a barbeque at our home. We had frequently held parties and barbeques in years past, games, food, booze, everything one would expect. This one was different; we did not intend for it to be different but it was. More than likely because I was now in a wheelchair. We all sat outside had a few drinks, cooked and talked. The most significant difference of this barbeque was the subject matter of the conversation. The subject was God. Is He real? Who is He? Etc. One of the guests brought a book by Thomas Merton. I didn't even know who Thomas Merton was. He was a Cistercian Monk that was very well known and had written many books. Needless to say his books are about God and his own life experiences and thoughts regarding that. I could not believe that this guest brought this book and that we were all involved in a free flowing conversation about God. Our barbeques had always been very loud with music and lots of drinking. This one was different. Everyone was interested in the conversation and everyone participated in the conversation. It was most unusual and most enjoyable, so enjoyable that we continued the barbeques every Sunday with the same guests for the rest of the summer.

Everyone really looked forward to these barbeques; the conversations were always lively and free flowing with all participating. Each week someone would bring a different book. We would peruse the book or the person most familiar with it would give a quick synopsis and we would discuss it. All of us were at our own personal stages of belief, faith and understanding of God. I was constantly plagued with doubt and questions that did not have definite concrete answers. I was always looking for proof. It isn't that I didn't believe in God. I was trying to understand God and was foolish enough to think that I was capable of that.

The conversations were always spiritual and intriguing but never had a final result. There was one exception to this. Therese had this absolute conviction that God was involved in every second of our lives. That was very difficult for me to accept. I always believed that we as human beings were in control of our lives and the outcome of our lives was in our own hands. God was sort of conceptual and abstract for me. I wanted to believe and I thought I believed but I wasn't certain in what I was trying to believe. She had this childlike faith that almost offended me. What kept me from rejecting her thoughts was her non-judgmental extraordinary gentleness. She did not force or push her thoughts and beliefs on anyone and she had this constant and unusual peace about her. This intrigued me and kept me interested in continuing these barbeque meetings.

It was late September the weather was getting too chilly and we stopped the barbeques. Therese went to see a priest in New Bedford for some advice the first Sunday that we did not have a barbeque. He sent her to a woman in New Hampshire for some further discussions. Therese was trying to find a Catholic sanctioned place to live and pray. The following weekend she went to New Hampshire to see that woman. When she returned she gave Joyce and me a little book that was written by St. Louis DeMontfort. She asked us both to read it and wanted to know what we thought of it. The woman in New Hampshire had a prayer group or cenacle and Therese wanted to know if we would like to start one. I instantly said yes, without first reading he book. Joyce read the book and said yes. Then I read the book and was sorry that I said yes.

The cenacle that she was asking us to start was much more involved than I thought. It required making a commitment to consecrate my life to Mary, the mother of Jesus. This consecration meant that you turned your life and everything in it over to Mary. This was much too deep and much too serious for me to do. I balked and stalled for several weeks by just never bring up the subject.

We were going to the adoration chapel almost every afternoon. In the fall of 1998 the Pope came to visit the USA in St. Louis, Mo. I was not particularly interested in that visit but in watching the news on T.V. it was covered every day so you really couldn't miss it. One evening while watching the coverage of this visit, I wondered, "who am I to question with all my questions"? This man is so well educated; he speaks eight or nine languages and has spent his life learning. He was so humble and so convicted of his thoughts. He spoke of love and goodness for all of humanity.

I did not even go to college, this man has spent his life learning; and I was questioning. Who was I and what credentials did I have to question? What did he know that I did not know? I could not wait to watch the news the next night and again the next night. I kept asking myself that question over and over again. I didn't get an answer but I knew it had to be something.

It occurred to me that if I did not have multiple sclerosis, I would not even be going to the chapel. I probably wouldn't even be going to church on Sundays. My concerns and priorities had always been associated with business, success and money. I prayed for some answers to my questions every day at the chapel. The most significant answer seemed to be faith. I was not going to understand this; I had to accept it in faith. Multiple sclerosis teaches you to accept many circumstances both new and difficult whether you like it or not. I had learned how to accept those circumstances; maybe I could learn how to accept faith.

My wife was ready to commit to this consecration and cenacle but I was still troubled by it. How could I turn my life and everything in it over to Mary, our Blessed Mother? It didn't even make sense to me. It seemed to be beyond me, I could not understand or accept the whole concept. Therese gave us two books that day; the second was titled "True Devotion to Mary". As I read it I remember thinking how wonderful this would all be, provided that you truly believed it. I was not sure what I believed, how could I do this?

We had a Sunday coming up with nothing planned and decided to spend it studying this book together. As we were doing this at our kitchen table several hours passed and there was a knock at our door. The door was right there in the kitchen so I just said, "come in". It was Therese. She was stunned that we were reading this book. It had not been discussed for a number of weeks. She did not want to intimidate or force us into it. I had not wanted to talk about it because I was afraid of it. Well we had to talk about it now, we had two of the books on our kitchen table and she had one in her hand. We all laughed, we were all surprised and we all wondered. We didn't all wonder, Therese didn't wonder; she said, "This may be God's will". I didn't like that, she always did that and I always said "oh sure, how do you know that"? This time I did think differently. I wanted to believe that it was in fact God's will. I wanted to believe this book but I was not sure. Therese had a scripture that a priest had given her to read. It was "Malachi 6:8", "Walk humbly with your God". We went to my computer to search out the scripture on the Internet. When I clicked on search, the box came on the screen with "Malachi 6:8" already typed in the box . . . . IT REALLY DID HAPPEN. That weak kneed feeling was now coupled with fear. We were all shocked and dumbfounded, how could this have possibly occurred? We still do not know but it did happen. I decided to make this commitment and to do this consecration.

Starting this cenacle required examining oneself and saying certain prayers for thirty-three days. Then, going to confession to a priest and reciting the consecration to our Blessed Mother in church. We were also not to solicit anyone to join this new cenacle; if anyone asked to join us we were to welcome him or her. By the way, this is all accomplished very privately. During these thirty-three days I learned and accepted as best I could that God was really in control of my life. Not me, as I had always thought. This was hard for me and at that time, I am not certain that I really accepted what I am telling you I accepted.

The first Sunday after we decided to commit to this Cenacle Therese wanted all of us to go and visit the priest in New Bedford. That was only about an hours driving time away so we decided to go. The priest was one of several Franciscan Monks that lived in the inner city of New Bedford, Ma. When we arrived there was no one there so we thought we would wait awhile hoping that they would return soon. The house that they lived in was on a corner and the front entrance was directly on the sidewalk. It was in a very old neighborhood not far from the waterfront. New Bedford of course was a thriving prosperous City one hundred years ago but not now. This neighborhood surely showed its age. I parked my car in the street just a few feet from the front door. We were parked with half the car in the street and half the car on the sidewalk and there was a telephone pole directly in front of us.

I am certain that at that moment a miracle occurred for me. As we waited I began to lose my eyesight. I could not believe what was happening. I was afraid to say anything to the girls and didn't. Looking out the window I could not see what was directly in front of me. I kept testing my eyes to see if this was really happening. It was a cloudy gray day the sky was actually more white than gray. I would lean forward to look out the windshield of the car so I could see only the white of the sky. There was nothing to see but white, as I did this my peripheral vision was like a rolling colored kaleidoscope, it was frightening. The telephone pole that was right in front of the car was there and then suddenly not there. My mind was almost in a panic. Am I losing my sight? I have to tell the girls. What do I say? How do I say it? I kept leaning forward to look up at the white sky and Therese laughingly asked me what I was doing. I was afraid to answer, I didn't want to tell but I knew that I had to tell them. I told them what had been happening to me while they were talking. Therese started to pray and Joyce had lots of questions and was very worried as she asked them. We all closed our eyes and started to say some "Hail Mary's" together. Therese and Joyce were also saying other prayers regarding my eyes. I kept my eyes closed during this time, which lasted about ten minutes. When I opened my eyes there in front of me was the telephone pole. I was ecstatic, I leaned forward to look up at the white sky and the kaleidoscope was gone. I could not believe it, I could see normally. Therese was not surprised, Joyce and I were very excited. We said thank you to God and started for home. The priests did not come back before we left. The drive home was most extraordinary. It was simply filled with thankfulness, excitement, humbleness and joy all at the same time. I now had a new thing to worry about and that was my eyesight. However, fortunately there have never been any eye problems since that time.

CHAPTER 6

Resistance Fades

Do not give your heart to your money,
Or say, "With this I am self-sufficient".

Ecclesiasticus 5:1

We lived about two hours away from a Monastery located in Massachusetts. We decided to go there on the last Sunday of the thirty-three days. Joyce and I had never been to a monastery and we were hoping to go to confession there. The services began at 6:40 A.M. It was December and when we arrived it was still dark.

Joyce and Therese went into the chapel that was there. My son John and I went into the choir section where the monks sat during their services. A sign at the entrance said "Monastic Enclosure, do not enter". Men were allowed to enter through this gate. The building was made of large stone blocks with a thick arched wood door. As John and I entered we saw the chapel where Joyce and Therese were and the altar to the right of that. Once inside we could see those in the chapel through a large picture window. Several candles were lit near the altar but the rest of the area was dark. I was in my wheelchair and as we entered we had to make a sharp turn to the right. As soon as we turned, there was a monk sitting alone praying. I felt like I had stepped back into the fifteenth century. We then had to go down a long arched corridor that was about twelve feet wide. There was a small stone altar at the end of the corridor; it seemed to be an altar for one person. There were several additional altars along the way. We had to turn left and were now at the back of the building at the rear wall. The sanctuary and choir area had extremely high ceilings with massive timbers, the entire area was very large and vast. There was another very large thick arched wood door, which I sat in front of in my wheelchair. Straight ahead about one hundred and fifty feet in front of me was the main altar. It was still dark; there was another monk sitting about ten feet away to my right. The altar had a large cross hanging over it suspended from the ceiling.

It is almost impossible to describe my thoughts and feelings. I was sitting there saying a prayer when a very old monk was slowly making his way to the corridor that I had just left. He had difficulty walking and used a cane. I was in the center of the building and the altar was directly in front of me. As the monk passed by me he got down on his knees to face the altar, struggled to get up and continued on his way. I knew that I was in a very holy place. This man was over seventy years of age. He had obviously spent his whole life praying for the likes of me and the rest of the human race. I'm not exactly sure how that made me think and feel, humble for sure and other mixed emotions.

My head was bowed, I continued to pray and was asking God to help me have faith and not to be so doubting and full of questions. When I looked up the sun was rising. Straight ahead in front of me on the opposite wall of the building, just behind the main altar was a large stained glass window. You could not see it in the dark but now the sun was coming up and brilliantly shining right through it. It was our Blessed Mother. I sat there wondering if I was being overly emotional or overly agnostic.

Many of the monks began to come into this choir area. As each one came into the large room and passed by the altar, they bowed toward it. Some got on their knees and prayed. There must have been seventy or eighty monks. Their ages ranged from mid-twenties-to quite elderly. It was now 6:40 A. M. They were all uniformly seated in their usual places. Five or six monks formed a circle in the center of the aisle and chanting by all the monks began. The chanting was beautiful, accompanied by an organ and lasted about twenty minutes. All of the monks wore an off white colored habit or robe with long billowy sleeves and hoods.

After several minutes of quiet, the chanting began again and a procession of priests entered the area on their way to the altar. The altar was about four or five steps up from the main floor. Most of the priests went up on the altar; several took what appeared to be their usual seats.

As I sat there, completely absorbed and mystified in what I was witnessing, I wondered, "What do these men know that I do not know?" I had the same thoughts that I had when I watched the Pope on T. V. several months previously. But now there were sixty or seventy men. Some of these monks had spent their lives reading and researching the Bible and other ancient writings. Who was I to question, what did I know about these matters? There was one thought in my mind that was in fact very clear. I was surely not in a position to be judging in any way.

As this Sunday Mass began one of the priests asked God to bless a large urn of water and to make it Holy. Several of the other priests took some of this holy water and sprinkled it on every person in attendance. For me it was an exceedingly moving moment. The Mass continued to be an extraordinary experience for me. Not that it was different from any other Mass, in any other Catholic Church that I had ever attended; it was not. What was different, definitely different was the presence of God that I felt. My questions were still there but somehow I knew there would now be answers to them.

When Mass was over we rejoined the girls outside at the front of the chapel. There were a number of people that had attended Mass mulling around talking and several monks. We asked one of the monks if we could go to confession. He said yes we could and pointed to a guesthouse that was a short distance away. He told us to knock on the door and someone would accommodate us. A priest answered the door with very sparkly happy eyes.

He was very gracious and asked us to come back in about an hour. He said a priest would then hear our confessions but it would not be he.

When we returned that same priest answered the door and told us that he would in fact be hearing our confessions. We were in the foyer of the guesthouse utilized by overnight guests that were on retreat. He wasn't quite sure where he was going to hear our confessions and led us to a small library-like office down the hall. We had a bit of difficulty getting me into the room due to the width of my wheelchair. We all laughed at this clumsiness and after a short struggle of folding and unfolding the wheelchair we got it into the room. The room was beautifully furnished with as I remember, several large windows. We sat face to face again as in that first confession that I made several months before.

During this confession I mentioned to the priest of my consistent nagging doubts and questions regarding God. Who is He? How do you know? I also told him of my thoughts regarding the Pope, this monastery, all the monks etc. He looked at me with the most profound confidence and assuredness and said look out the window." As I did this he said, "Do you think this is all an accident? Do you think this is all from The Big Bang" ? That is preposterous. Look at the grass, the trees, look how green they are, it's winter. Pine trees are green in winter, for us, God loves us. He made them for us. Spring comes and there are thousands of different colored flowers and trees. Look at all the animals that live out there, look at the sky, and look at the veins in your wrists, look at the systems within your body. God made it all. God loves us. All good things come from God. If we take the time to look we will find Him. He has made it very clear that He is here." This priest seemed to understand with uncanny accuracy exactly where I was in my own mind regarding all of my thoughts and questions. He said, "God loves us and wants us to share His kingdom with Him. He has a plan, we are all part of that plan and He has given us the plan." He gave me absolution and for my penance he told me to go before the Blessed Sacrament at our church at home. He said to tell God what I just told him and to give the problem of my doubts and questions to Jesus. He also said to be still, be at peace and to trust in God's Grace. This confession and conversation lasted about an hour and a half.

The girls also went to confession. As we getting ready to leave that very first priest that we asked about confession waved to us from a short distance away and came over to our car. He asked if our needs were met. We thanked him and replied yes. He was pleased and happy to hear of that. We left the Monastery about 1:30 P. M. When we got home we went to the adoration chapel to do our penance. I did as I was told and just sat there thinking about the day. It had been a very unusual and extraordinary day for me. It was the first time in my life, that I had spent an entire day in church. I must say that I felt the most profound peace and contentment. It was as if everything in my body and my life was calm, peaceful and settled. I have always been a happy contented individual but this was different, almost like I had stepped up to a higher plain that I did not previously know existed.

We continued to go to our chapel daily. It became a most important part of our day. I couldn't believe it, I was never interested in church or God and now I was going every day. The monks and the monastery were always on my mind; we couldn't wait to go back again. We returned to the monastery several times during the next few weeks. It was Christmas time and the services there were very special.

Six or seven weeks passed. I called the priest at the monastery and asked if we could come for confession again. He was most welcoming and said surely. This time he arranged to meet us in a much more easily accessible room. After my confession I asked him about some difficulties that we were having with our oldest son and our oldest daughter. My son had two boys that we very seldom would see or visit. My MS restricted me from getting into their house and due to these other difficulties they did not come to our house. My daughter was single and for whatever the reasons we didn't see her either. He told me to go to the Blessed Sacrament at our chapel and to again ask God to help us with this problem. I did that and the next day my son brought our grandchildren to our store for a visit. He brought them again the day after that, and again the day after that. In the space of one week we saw more of our son and grandchildren than we had in the past five years! My daughter also started to come visit us three or four mornings a week for coffee. Both of these circumstances began a new dialogue with each of these children. The visits became and remain more and more frequent. The difficulties and/or differences have been slowly set aside. We have a new atmosphere of tolerance with our differences. We all now seem to be aware that we are all individuals, we are all different, we all love one another and all we have to do is accept that.

These changes that happened so quickly and my constant desire to go to our chapel made me both curious and perplexed. I could see answers to prayers occurring but at the same time those answers created more questions. Are these just coincidences or are they answers to prayer? How do you know? Then I would feel guilty about my questions and my doubts. Was I being ungrateful, were my prayers being answered? Was I rationalizing those answers and why was I constantly looking for proof? The priest at the monastery said to give the prayers and problems to God, and trust. Why didn't I trust? I did when I was at the monastery, I did when I was in our chapel but when I left those places the doubts and questions would start.

I started to read the Bible and two startling revelations occurred. The first was a passage that I read in the Old Testament. Isaiah 7:14 Specifically states: "The Lord himself, therefore, will give you a sign. It is this: the maiden is with child and will soon give birth to a son whom she will call Immanuel." Then in the New Testament, Matthew 1:23 "The Virgin will conceive and give birth to a son and they will call him Emmanuel." The Old Testament was written several thousand years before the New Testament, and the verses were identical.

The second was in the book of Genesis. Chapter 14, verse 18 "Melchizedek king of Salem brought bread and wine; he was a priest of God Most High." Keep in mind that this was written several thousand years before this; Hebrews chapter 5 verse 6; "You are a priest of the order of Melchizedek, and forever". This priest Melchizedek several thousand years earlier brought as an offering to God, bread and wine. Now Jesus tells his disciples to take this bread and eat it, it is my body, which will be given up for you. He too then uses wine and tells them to drink it; it is his blood, which will be shed for them. Do this in memory of me.

These two findings were most impressive and intense for me. They aroused my curiosity and created additional questions. How could these two identical passages be identical? They were written several thousand years apart from one another. Is this all true and is it really as simple as it appears? The priest said it was and that if we asked God for the Grace to accept it He would give us the faith to do so. He told me to sit before the Blessed Sacrament to ask for faith and to acknowledge my doubts. I read a famous simple prayer and said it daily in front of the Blessed Sacrament; "Jesus thank you for my belief, help my unbelief". I bought a little book called "The wisdom of the Apostles". The first verse in the book is: "IF ANY OF YOU IS LACKING IN WISDOM, ASK GOD, WHO GIVES TO ALL GENEROUSLY AND UNGRUDGINGLY, AND IT WILL BE GIVEN TO YOU. BUT ASK IN FAITH, NEVER DOUBTING, FOR THE ONE WHO DOUBTS IS LIKE A WAVE OF THE SEA, DRIVEN AND TOSSED BY THE WIND." JAMES 1; 5-6. That was me, I was always doubting and I always ran hot and cold. Up and down back and forth.

We started our cenacle and we met once a week on Thursday evenings. One of the elements of criteria involving the cenacle was that you were not to ask anyone to join it. Others could join but they had to ask us, we were not to ask them. Therese had that same simple, innocent, accepting confidence that the priest did. That all the Monks did, that the Pope did, that the priests in our church did, that my wife did. Why didn't I? I believed in God but I wasn't sure who He was. I was not confident or certain in what I believed. I was a bit unsure of this cenacle and the commitment that it required. As it progressed my thoughts began to change and I looked forward to it. When our cenacle started I was not particularly enthusiastic about spending two or three hours in the evening praying. In fact I wanted to cancel it before we even began. But it was not cancelled. After the first one I had all of those feelings of peace and contentment. I was surprised and began to notice some striking similarities regarding church, God and multiple sclerosis. It has been over three years since we started our cenacle and we now have a Priest and a former Cistercian Monk with us. Both of them asked us if they could join our Cenacle, we did not ask them.

Multiple Sclerosis, with its difficulties, teaches one to accept the difficulties whether you like it or not. When that acceptance is genuine and without reservation, there comes a peace. I don't mean giving in and I don't mean giving up, I mean just accepting what is. It took me a number of years to get to that point of acceptance with MS. When I did and it changes frequently, you get peace of mind, even contentment. When you have done your best, truly your best, you cannot do more. Knowing that gives you peace. I was experiencing a similar peace of mind during and after our cenacle and when I went to our chapel. The priest at the monastery told me to pray for faith and that it was a God given Grace.

I began to understand that I was not going to understand, I had to accept, I had to have faith. I think most of us human beings at one time or another are presumptuous enough to believe that we are capable of understanding God. The faith that I had always known in the past wasn't really faith. I had always been uncertain of God, of prayers and my faith had been a last resort of not really knowing and having definite answers.

My thoughts regarding God, faith and praying began to change and when I prayed I had an unusual feeling of peace, calmness and confidence. It was a contentment that is most difficult to describe. It was a satisfied feeling that is rather extraordinary because I didn't do anything to get it. It was not a feeling of accomplishment, not a feeling of victory or anything like that, just peaceful. It was also a new and dissimilar peace to what I had previously experienced. Confidence and assurance would best describe it. Interestingly, it became most noticeable when it was not with me. It felt as though something was missing, like I forgot something. It felt unsettled and sort of uneasy. It made me wonder where the peace that I had, had gone and I wanted it back.

It became apparent to me that when these peaceful thoughts and feelings were missing, I was struggling with a situation and attempting to resolve it myself without trusting in God. It could have been a financial problem, a business problem, family problem, health problem. During these times I would most often neglect my daily prayers being so intent on solving the difficulty. When I let go of the problem and when I returned to my prayers, the peace would return. Oftentimes letting go of the problem occurred only because there was no other choice. I did not see or have a solution. So I let go, almost as if being forced to let go because of no other options. It was exactly as a quote that I once read by Alexander M. Schindler, a Jewish Rabbi. "Hold fast, and let go: understand this paradox, and you stand at the very gate of wisdom."

Easter was coming soon and we decided to go to the monastery for the services on Holy Thursday. The services began at 3:00 P. M. That meant in order to get there on time we had to leave by 12:30 P. M. Which also meant that we had to close our business early, before noon. We had never done that before but we did it for the first time. It was most unusual for me to be so continually interested in God, going to church and praying so often.

We arrived at the monastery about 2:30 P. M. there were already more people there than usual. People kept coming in and by 3:00 P. M. the two chapels and choir area were filled. During Easter week men and women are permitted in the choir area so we all sat together in that area. There were no monks in their usual places but you could hear them chanting elsewhere in the monastery. Part of the ceremony had begun and was taking place outside of the sanctuary and altar area. That part of the ceremony was only for the monks. The chanting was coming closer and closer and a procession with all the monks entered and they took their usual places. It was quite beautiful to see and hear for me. The Holy Thursday ceremony was a reenactment of Jesus washing the feet of His apostles, which we did not see and Benediction of the Blessed Sacrament in which we did participate. The ceremony ended with all in attendance holding a lighted candle in procession to the Tabernacle where the Blessed Sacrament is kept.

This was a very beautiful and moving ceremony for all of us and we all wanted to return for Easter Mass on Sunday. Easter services were to begin at 3:00 A. M. We arrived for those services at 2:15 A. M. and entered the monastery. The monastery was dimly lit as usual but what was unusual was the number of people that were already there. The place was full. Once again we were all permitted into the choir area. Shortly after we took our places the dim lights were turned off and the candles were extinguished. It was pitch black. It was so dark that you could not see anything and I mean anything. There was absolute silence, you could hear a pin drop. I did not know what to think or do, I was sort of bewildered. It was most extraordinary with all these people sitting in total silence in complete pitch-black darkness. After what seemed to be a long time and I don't know how long it was, I nodded my head and said an "Our Father".

I picked up my head and straight ahead on the altar there seemed to be a figure of a man. At that same exact instant, my peripheral vision to my right saw a similar figure. My heart started to pound, I quickly turned my head to the right to look. There was nothing, I turned to look back at the altar and the figure was there. Now my peripheral vision to the right saw the figure again. I turned again to the right to look and there was nothing. I turned again toward the altar and now there were two figures, one taller than the other. It was still dark and these figures were like glows, they were just slightly lighter than the dark. One appeared to be a man, the other a woman. I couldn't believe it; I kept turning my head back and forth. Each time I turned to the right there was nothing until I turned to the altar and it was there again. The two figures on the altar did not disappear; the one to my right did when I looked directly at it. The figures on the altar were about one hundred feet in front of me, the figure to my right was only about ten or twelve feet from me. The last time that I turned to the right to look, the figure disappeared and I heard a soft swishing noise and felt a breeze on my face. To say that I was in a state of complete trauma would be an understatement.

I do not recall if the monks were chanting or if the services had begun while this occurred, I was so caught up with these images that I don't remember. I do remember that it was still dark and that there was a significant period of silence after this happened. As I sat there bewildered and wondering with this, two thoughts became quite clear. Trust in God and Faith in God. This entire relationship with God that I had struggled with and questioned for so long was quite different from whatever it was that I expected. I was filled with contrasting emotions. I was fearful but yet at the same time I had an incredible peace. I was filled with questions and yet there seemed to be unknowing inexplicable satisfactory answers. There was no need for a definite logical explanation; it could not exist.

The lights came back on, the services continued and Easter Mass was celebrated. When Mass was over I asked a man that was sitting next to me if he heard or saw anything during the earlier darkness. He responded with a smile and said, "You have very good eyes". I asked again and he just smiled. My wife Joyce and Therese came over to me, we were all very excited. Several of the monks came back into the choir area, which was filled with people, to wish those still in the area, happy Easter. Everyone was mulling around wishing each other a happy Easter. Joyce asked me if I felt anything earlier in that darkness. I told her what I had seen and heard and the breeze that blew into my face. She saw the same images and felt something brush against her hair. Therese had also seen it. I was almost speechless and looking for some sort of explanation but I knew that there wouldn't be any. I was reluctant to ask anyone else any questions and did not. Most of the people began to leave with the exception of those that appeared to be friends or relatives of the monks. We also left and went home to celebrate Easter Sunday.

CHAPTER 7

Divine Guidance

With all your soul hold the Lord in awe,
And revere His priests.
With all your might love Him who made you,
And do not abandon His ministers.
Fear the Lord and honor the priest
And give him the portion enjoined on you:

Ecclesiasticus 7:29-33

While we were prospering at the Café', the stocks that I bought when we sold the deli were doing poorer and poorer. I bought them in June of 1996 at in excess of ninety thousand dollars and by September of 1997 they were worth less than ten thousand dollars. To say that I was sick over it is the understatement of the decade. Other than our house and Café they were our only assets. All four of the stocks had declined significantly and had remained so until November of 2000.

I used to go home from the Café' every day and check them on our computer. Hmm . . . . maybe that's why they stayed so low. Then in November of 2000 they started to show a significant amount of activity. Each of the stocks price slowly started rise and their volume increased daily on the over-the-counter stock exchange.

What had become a depressing burden of checking the stocks every day now became an exciting daily event. I couldn't wait to get home every day to check the stocks. Then in early February one of the stocks: CITN went from seventy cents a share to $4.50 a share in three days. I has ten thousand shares and sold it. The next three or four days the other three stocks basically did the same thing. In the course of one week I sold all the stocks. Not only did we recover all the money we invested . . . . we made a profit of twenty seven thousand dollars. The most incredible part of this story is that within one week all four of those stocks were back down to being worth less than ten thousand dollars. How do I explain this . . . . I can't, coincidence? I don't think so. Lucky, certainly but I don't think that either. Must therefore be an answer to prayer . . . . What else could it be ?

We paid off most of our mortgage and decided to close the Café' for three weeks and go to Florida to visit Joyce's Parents. The timing was perfect, it was March and business was a bit slower this time of year.

The Internal Revenue Service had filed a Federal Tax lien against us for $37,000. in 1997 due to the sale of the deli. I could figure out how to pay this while in Florida.

While we were in Florida we were impressed by the number of really nice and reasonably priced over fifty five communities. We were really was not particularly fond of Florida. We both liked the change of seasons and had an attachment to New England. However, there were several very positive reasons to consider a move there.

First and foremost was the fact that Joyce's family lived there. Her parents, her brother and his wife, as well as several aunts and uncles were there as well. We had been away from her family for over twenty years and she only saw them on rare occasions. This would be an opportunity for her to see them and enjoy their company on a regular basis. We could also realize enough proceeds from the sale of our house in Cape Cod to pay the tax lien and pay cash for a home in one of these communities.

From a strictly financial point of view, this made the most sense. Then again, we did have some concerns. This was a big step and Joyce's Mother cautioned us to really think it out. When they did it she took a long time to adjust and really missed her kids not being close by. She also said that she would not do it again. We would have the same situation. In addition the heat would be a problem for me, folks with multiple sclerosis do not do well in the heat. But I spoke to a few friends that lived in Florida and they loved it. They said that everything was air conditioned in the hot months from June-November.

Living in Cape Cod might actually have been more problematic than Florida. From October to May I had to stay inside most of the time. In Florida it would only be from June to October. We pained over making this decision for a year or two.

We still had not made a decision to move and struggled once again as to whether or not we should sell the Café. We were getting busier and busier and that put an unreasonable burden on Joyce. That was a frustrating situation for both of us. The whole idea of being in business is to succeed by doing more and more business but for us that was a predicament. Due to the limitations that multiple sclerosis caused for me there were only certain duties that I could do. Everything else that had to be done fell on Joyce. Selling the Café also presented another problem, how would we support ourselves? The strongest reason to move to Florida turned out to be mostly financial. If we sold our house here there would be enough proceeds to buy a home there and have amount left. Together with my Social Security we would be able to live decently. We were going round and round with this decision, one day it was yes the next day it was no. On the other hand if we stayed in Cape Cod there was enough equity in our house to make it handicap accessible and live relatively comfortable. We had two major decisions to make. In the midst of trying to make these decisions we were trying to determine what God's will was for our lives. And just like in the old days before I returned to church, I was beleaguered with frustration and confusion. Then one Sunday we went to Mass and these decisions were constantly on both of our minds. When we came out of church there in the sky once again was an enormous rainbow. It was gigantic and spanned the entire sky from horizon to horizon. We looked at each other is disbelief. We lived just about five miles from the church and the rainbow remained in the sky for the entire ride home. For the second time the rainbow pushed us just enough to make one of the decisions. We decided that day to sell the Café. Not only did we make the decision but the decision was filled with the most indescribable peace for both of us. We stayed with the new owner for a few months but Joyce developed a problem with her back that required surgery. After her recovery we seriously began to consider the move to Florida. This decision was not as difficult to make for us and ultimately decided to make the move.

Then several astonishing events occurred. We put our house on the market and sold it in a relatively short period of time. We had several months to wait before the closing so we made arrangements to take another trip to Florida. We still did not have a place to live there.

During one of the conversations that Joyce had with her mother Joyce mentioned to her how she was going to miss the adoration chapel at our church. Her Mother said that a friend of hers mentioned that they were building a new church in North Fort Myers. She said that the new church was a mission church sponsored by a larger church located in Fort Myers. A mission church is a satellite for a sparsely populated area. My mother-in-law lived in Cape Coral, about twelve miles away from North Fort Myers.

We drove to Florida, I drive with hand controls. Being in a wheelchair flying was a problem for me in case I had to go to the bathroom. We took our time, stayed over two nights and arrived in Florida on a Saturday morning. Heh, heh . . . . I thought we were there and told Joyce to call her Mother to tell her we would be there in a couple of hours. She said "Oh no you won't your still five and a half hours away". I never really realized how big and long the State of Florida is in a car. Be that as it may, five and a half hours later we came to the exit off Interstate 75 for Cape Coral. The exit led us to Route 41 South. (Rt. 41 is a North-South highway on the West coast of the state that used to be the main artery before the Interstate system was built)

We were in a rural area and proceeded South for several miles. Then we spot an obscure sign that says; "St Therese Catholic Church". Were in farmland and an unpopulated area. We drive in and down a long driveway and there stands a new church. There are no cars in the large parking lot but there is another sign with an arrow pointing and the sign says . . . "Adoration Chapel".

Well, to say we were surely surprised is an understatement. We went into the church, there was no one there but it was open. It was just recently completed and behind the Altar we found the adoration chapel. We were actually a bit stunned at finding this and it being our first stop and an accidental stop at that. On second thought, hardly accidental. We stayed in the chapel, said some thankful prayers and left wondering how and why this managed to be our first stop in Florida. As soon as we left not more than four hundred yards down the road we passed an over fifty five community called "Pine Lakes".

We proceeded to Joyce's Mother's house and spent the next five or six days looking at various over fifty five communities. Quite unsuccessfully, we were looking for either a handicapped accessible home or one that could easily be converted. That was quite a hectic process for us especially for Joyce. When we travel we bring two portable ramps so I have access to get into wherever we are going.

As we looked at these homes Joyce would go in to look around and if she thought that it might be suitable she would come back to the car to get me. Then she would have to take the ramps out of the car and then set them up to get in the house. After we looked at the house she would then remove the ramps and put them back into the car. We had to do this for each house that I was going to see. Fortunately, we had a van and that made it a bit easier.

We basically knew where we were going to look. I had perused a number of communities before we left Cape Cod utilizing the Internet. We found several possibilities but nothing with which we were particularly impressed. We only had one more day before we were heading back to Cape Cod. I had pre-arranged appointments to see most of the homes so we did not get to see anything at "Pine Lakes". When I made those appointments I did not even know that "Pine Lakes" was there. So the last day we stopped into the office at "Pine Lakes" to look at the community. They were very busy and we had to wait. Finally a salesman came over to us and apologized for keeping us waiting so long. He said that he had several appointments but gave us the address's of two homes that we could look at by ourselves. He called the owners to advise them that we would be coming.

We went to the first house and Joyce went in to look at it. She came back a few minutes later extremely excited. She said "Tom, you have got to see this house it is magnificent". We took the ramps out of the van and set them up for me to get into the house. As I entered the front door I just could not believe my eyes. The house was beautiful, pristine and wide open. The kitchen was nearly new, the living room and dining room were spacious and the bedrooms were enormous. The house had two full bathrooms, was central air conditioned and had a garage. It was also easily accessible and only required a ramp to be built. This was really encouraging and even exciting. One of the reasons we were considering the move was that our house in Cape Cod was very confining and inaccessible for me. This house was just the opposite.

We thanked the owners for allowing us to view their home and went back to the office. We made an offer to buy and made a deposit. The salesman said that he would call us later that day. Several hours later he called us to tell us that our offer was accepted and that we bought ourselves a house. We were ecstatic and heading home the next day. THE HOUSE WAS LESS THAN A QUARTER OF A MILE FROM ST. THERESE'S CATHOLIC CHURCH AND ADORATION CHAPEL.

CHAPTER 8

Hold fast . . . and . . . Let go

Do not try to understand things that are too difficult for you,
Or try to discover what is beyond your powers.
Concentrate on what has been assigned you,
You have no need to worry over mysteries.
Do not mettle with matters that are beyond you;
What you have been taught already exceeds the scope of the human mind.
For many have been mislead by their own presumption,
And wrong-headed opinions have warped their ideas.

Ecclesiasticus 3:21-26

We returned to Cape Cod and started to make the arrangements for the move. The first thing to do was to contact a mover and set a date. We had to close in Florida on April 22, that gave us plenty of time it was still only January. To move the entire contents of our house in Cape Cod turned out to be incredibly expensive and was just not worth it. So we decided to sell most of the furniture and just move our bedroom set and several other favorite pieces of furniture. In spite of that we still wound up having to pack over one hundred boxes of clothing, china, etc. and everything else that goes along with a home. We called in a company that handles estate sales to liquidate the furniture and the other things that we were not going to take to Florida.

We packed a few boxes everyday and after six or seven weeks we were almost ready. The people handling the estate sale came in and priced everything for two days. They had an estimate of value and their commission was based on that value. It was only an estimate and the actual commission would be determined by the total dollars realizes from the sale.

Now everything is all set. We have a sale date, we have a closing date in Cape Cod, we have a moving date and we have a closing date in Florida. Two days before the estate sale the deal on the house in Cape Cod falls apart, the buyers back out. Clearly, we now have some serious troubles. I could not cancel the estate sale without paying the commission based on the estimate. Our house is no longer sold and we needed the proceeds in order to purchase the home in Florida. If we did not close on the house in Florida we would lose our ten per cent deposit. We also did not want to lose the house in Florida.

We went instantly to our lawyer to make sure that the buyer would forfeit their deposit. Our lawyer said that under normal circumstances the answer would be yes but there was a problem with our deed. It was a minor problem but one that entitled the buyer to get the deposit back. That problem meant that we would have to sue them and he said that we would lose the suit.

So we put the house back on the market and proceeded with the estate sale. We were crushed and spent a lot of time at the chapel praying and wondering what the heck was going on?? Talk about frustration and confusion, we were certainly living that.

We decided to contact a second mortgage company to take out a second mortgage with enough funds to buy the house in Florida. Then when we sold the Cape Cod house we would pay it back. That is what we did and after the house was appraised the mortgage man came to our house to execute the final papers. He came to our home about 5:00PM one afternoon to do this.

We were all sitting around our kitchen table and the phone rang. I answered the phone, it was my brother. He asked what I was doing. He already knew what had happed to the sale of the house. I told him what we were doing with the mortgage company. He said; "Don't do anything, don't sign anything".

I was sitting there with the mortgage man right in front of me. My brother is telling me not to do anything and I have this guy sitting right there in front of me waiting for me to sign. We let me tell you, talk about pressure cookers, I was in one of them. My brother said to stall this guy until tomorrow and that he would talk to me later.

I hung up the phone and asked him if we could finish this tomorrow morning. He agreed and we made another appointment for 11:00AM the next day. My brother called me back and said that he would make some calls and call me back the next morning.

The next day at 8:00AM my brother called. He asked how much money would I need to proceed in Florida. I said; "It's hard to tell, it depends on how long it takes for us to sell our house, probably about fifty five or sixty thousand dollars. My brother then said; "I don't have the money but I can get it, I'll call you back in ten minutes". A few minutes later the phone rang, it was my brother. He said; "I got the money, $75,000. just in case you need a little extra. But the man I got it from will only give it to me and I have to hand it to you. I'm leaving N. J. at 10:00AM this morning and driving to Cape Cod. I'll see you around 3:00PM . . . Make sure you have a two pound lobster". I said; "Bob we can do this electronically just go to the bank". He said: "No we can't, I'll see you at three o'clock and I'm driving right back . . . . don't forget the lobster".

There I sat dumbfounded. Someone that I don't even know is lending me $75,000. No collateral, no mortgages, no notes, no nothing, I couldn't believe it. I called the mortgage man to cancel our eleven 0'clock appointment. I then called the Swan River Fish Market and ordered three cooked lobsters to be picked up at 4:00PM.

My brother arrived just about on time. He explained that this man was a business partner of his. And that he trusted him and if he trusted him he could also trust his brother. He then handed me a bank check made out to me for $75,000. We went to the bank to deposit the check, picked up the lobsters and came home. Joyce was a tearful basket case, picking on her lobster in disbelief. We finished the lobsters, Bob said "When you sell your house just pay him back, no interest". He got in his car and drove home to New Jersey.

In the meantime our house was being shown and several weeks later we received a new offer and reached another agreement. This new contract called for a closing of the Cape house to occur in June. In was now March and the closing on the house in Florida was scheduled for April 22. That was okay, our lawyer advised that we did not have to be here, it could all be done in the mail. So we were ready to go, the estate sale had taken place and there was nothing left to do.

Then the most mysterious and beyond belief thing happened. We got a letter in the mail, the return address on the envelope read; "Barnstable County Registrar of Deeds." I opened the envelope and lo and behold inside the envelope was a "Release of a Federal Tax Lien in the amount of $37,000."

That lien was over five years old and with the interest added it amounted to close to $50,000. I could not believe my eyes. I called my lawyer and asked him if this was for real, I just couldn't believe it. He said to fax it over to him and that he would call me after he looked at it. An hour or so later he called back and said that it was for real. The lien had been released and I no longer owed the money. We had expected to pay the lien when the Cape Cod house closed. Now we did not owe it . . . . I felt like we just won the lottery.

Our attorney was full of questions, I was full of questions, how and why did this happen. Me being me . . . no questions, no nuttin . . . don't look a gift horse in the mouth. We still do not know how or why. We made the move to Florida and closed on the new home there. Several weeks later we sold the house in Cape Cod and paid back the $75,000.

There is one other example of what is truly a miracle that has been left out so far. It has been left out due to my paining over whether or not I have the courage to include it.

As mentioned earlier in 1974 I made a lot of money, at least for us it was a lot of money. By 1976 most of that money was gone. My wife was working for a group of gynecological doctors. We were concerned about her getting pregnant and we went together to see about me getting a vasectomy. As we were listening to the doctor explain the procedure the most uncomfortable feeling came over me. It was an uneasy and disturbing feeling. It was not fear but just a very unsettling and noticeable unmerciful time. I looked at my wife and said "I don't think we should do this".

Well wouldn't you know that sure enough within about six months my wife got pregnant. I was totally distraught, we could not afford another child. We needed my wife's job and this would mean the end to that. I was beside myself trying to figure out what to do and how to get out of this. However, the only way out was an abortion which had recently become legal. I mentioned that to her and she was aghast that I could even think of such thoughts.

Without telling her I called an abortion clinic and made an appointment for her three weeks down the line. This gave me three weeks to convince her that we had to do this in order to survive financially.

I spent the next two weeks or so rationalizing and justifying why we had to do this. Joyce was never one to argue and just listened to my ranting and raving about it. When she did respond she would mention that it was something that God would definitely not want us to do.

Finally after discussions over this every day I agreed to call a Christian TV program. There was no doubt in my mind that I could convince anyone that we were justified in making this decision. I picked up the phone and made the call. The person on the other end was most sympathetic, understanding and listened to me carefully and intently. He then asked me if he could pray with me. I said ok and as he prayed that uneasy and comfortable feeling came back. It was a strong and powerful feeling that suddenly became a peaceful and comfortable in an instant. My thoughts turned to enthusiasm and excitement. I knew almost instantly that there would be no abortion. I thanked the man, hung up the phone and told my wife . . . . She cried.

When we had our first three kids I sat in a waiting room at the hospital and waited for the baby to be born. This time I was in the delivery room with my wife and the doctor and nurses. That was certainly a very foreign environment for me. Here was my naked wife lying on a table with two male doctors, me and several nurses. She is in labor, I am trying to comfort her and everyone else is extremely busy. As I was looking into her eyes, (she had no drugs or pain killers), she is in agony . . . glancing up I see the two windows to the door and just wanted to run through the door and get out of there. But I can't do that, she needs me now. Breathe, breathe, breathe . . . now the doctor says; "You better come look now or you are going to miss it." So I go to the other end of the table and what I see is shocking. The baby's head is coming out and I can't believe my eyes. In several seconds the whole bloody baby is out. The doctor asks me if I would like to cut the cord . . . . Oh my God, I don't remember if I did or not. The doctor puts the baby on Joyce's stomach, all is quiet now and the room has been darkened. After several seconds the baby's eyes just pop open . . . . and she is looking straight at me. I cried in disbelief. Everyone in the room is now happy, smiling and laughing. It is surreal to me, he nurse cleans up the baby and the doc asks Joyce if she would like to walk to her room. (She had no drugs) I couldn't believe it, she did.

Jennifer, our new baby has now grown to be twenty nine years old. Throughout her life she has brought love, inspiration and enthusiasm for life every single day. She was seven years old when I was diagnosed with multiple sclerosis and has been an inspiration and motivation ever since. Through that time when diagnosed with MS Jennifer has been something of a paradox.

She has always had this gentle way of acceptance of my MS troubles and at the same time pushing the envelope to endure and proceed through those difficulties. Many of those problems too numerous to mention might not have been conquered without her. The bond that started that night on the phone is still intact and stronger than ever. Thank God for Jennifer.

I saved this for last because I was ashamed at what I might have done without God's involvement. Hopefully it may help someone in similar circumstances. Jennifer's birthday is August 15th . . . . no small coincidence. August 15 is the Feast of the Assumption . . . . that is the celebration of the day that The Virgin Mary was taken up to heaven. This was not very meaningful or significant to me at the time. However, thankfully God has seen fit to give me some Faith, Enlightenment and Wisdom . . . it is surely significant to me now.

Throughout human history this human race of ours has worshipped and/or prayed to a God or Gods. There were idols worshiped, then gods for everything else that existed. There were gods everywhere, gods of the sea, gods of the sky, gods of the mountains, gods of the valleys, etc. No matter where or when the evidence that proves this is overwhelming and indisputable.

That would certainly indicate that we are ALL and have ALL been born with an inner instinct to that effect. That instinct is just as natural as any living creature's instinct is to survive. How else can humanity's attachment to worship and prayer be explained. The fact of the matter is that it cannot be explained.

The archaeological digs and sites that have taken place in the past and that continue to this day confirm that the old testament of the Bible is reliable. The timing is accurate, the events are accurate, the places are accurate, the individuals involved are accurate. Happenstance? Hardly. Coincidence? Not likely, the odds of that being the case are not even measurable. The books of the Bible were written by human authors and it is not even known who some of these authors were.

All of this brings us to some astonishing things to consider and they are; the Prophecies regarding Jesus in the Old Testament. There are over fifty of those Prophecies.

II Samuel 7:12-16 . . . . *When your days are over and you rest with your fathers, I will raise up your offspring to succeed you, who will come from your own body, and I will establish his kingdom. He is the one who will build a house for my Name, and I will establish the throne of his kingdom forever. I will be his father, and he will be my son. When he does wrong, I will punish him with the rod of men, with floggings inflicted by men. But my love will never be taken away from him, as I took it away from Saul, whom I removed from before you. Your house and your kingdom will endure forever before me; your throne will be established forever (NIV).*

Psalms 89:3-4 . . . . "I have sworn unto David my servant, Thy seed will I establish for ever, and build up thy throne to all generations

Isaiah 9:6, 7; 11:1 . . . . *"For a child will be born to us, a son will be given to us; And the government will rest on His shoulders; And His name will be called Wonderful Counselor, Mighty God, Eternal Father, Prince of Peace." (Isaiah 9:6).*

Of the increase of his government and peace there shall be no end, upon the throne of David, and upon his kingdom, to order it, and to establish it with judgment and with justice from henceforth even for ever. The zeal of the LORD of hosts will perform this.

Isaiah
Chapter 11

1

But a shoot shall sprout from the stump of Jesse, and from his roots a bud shall blossom.

2

The spirit of the LORD shall rest upon him: a spirit of wisdom and of understanding, A spirit of counsel and of strength, a spirit of knowledge and of fear of the LORD, and his delight shall be the fear of the LORD. Not by appearance shall he judge, nor by hearsay shall he decide,

4

But he shall judge the poor with justice, and decide aright for the land's afflicted. He shall strike the ruthless with the rod of his mouth, and with the breath of his lips he shall slay the wicked.

5

Justice shall be the band around his waist, and faithfulness a belt upon his hips.

6

Then the wolf shall be a guest of the lamb, and the leopard shall lie down with the kid; The calf and the young lion shall browse together, with a little child to guide them.

7

The cow and the bear shall be neighbors, together their young shall rest; the lion shall eat hay like the ox.

8

The baby shall play by the cobra's den, and the child lay his hand on the adder's lair.

9

There shall be no harm or ruin on all my holy mountain; for the earth shall be filled with knowledge of the LORD, as water covers the sea.

10

On that day, The root of Jesse, set up as a signal for the nations, The Gentiles shall seek out, for his dwelling shall be glorious.

11

Micah 5:2 . . . . 2 "But you, Bethlehem Ephrathah, though you are small among the clans [a] of Judah, out of you will come for me one who will be ruler over Israel, whose origins [b] are from of old, from ancient times.

Hosea 11:1 . . . . When Israel was a child I loved him, out of Egypt I called my son.

Isaiah 9:1, 2 . . . . The people who walked in darkness have seen a great light; Upon those who dwelt in the land of gloom a light has shone.

Isaiah 40: 3-5 . . . . **A voice of one calling: "In the desert prepare the way for the LORD; make straight in the wilderness a highway for our God. Every valley shall be raised up, every mountain and hill made low; the rough ground shall become level, the rugged places a plain. And the glory of the LORD will be revealed, and all mankind together will see it. For the mouth of the LORD has spoken."**

Malachi 3:1, ... 1 "See, I am going to send My messenger, [A] and he will clear the way before Me. [B] Then the Lord you seek [C] will suddenly come to

His temple, (D) the Messenger of the covenant you desire—see, He is coming," says the LORD of Hosts.

Genesis 35: 19-20 .... Because thy servant hath found grace before thee, and thou hast magnified thy mercy, which thou hast shown to me, in saving my life, and I cannot escape to the mountain, lest some evil seize me, and I die. There is this city here at hand, to which I may flee, it is a little one, and I shall be saved in it: is it not a little one, and my soul shall live?

Isaiah 58:6 .... "Is not this the fast that I choose:to loose the bonds of wickedness,to undo the straps of the yoke,to let the oppressed go free,and to break every yoke?

Isaiah 61:1 .... The Year of the LORD's Favor

1 The Spirit of the Sovereign LORD is on me, because the LORD has anointed me to preach good news to the poor. He has sent me to bind up the brokenhearted, to proclaim freedom for the captives and release from darkness for the prisoners, [a]

Isaiah 42;1-4 .... **Behold, My Servant, whom I uphold; My chosen one in whom My soul delights. I have put My Spirit upon Him; He will bring forth justice to the nations. He will not cry out or raise His voice, nor make His voice heard in the street. A bruised reed He will not break, and a dimly burning wick He will not extinguish; He will faithfully bring forth justice. He will not be disheartened or crushed, until He has established justice in the earth; and the coastlands will wait expectantly for His law. (Isaiah 42:1-4)**

Isaiah 53:4-6 ....

4 Surely he took up our infirmities and carried our sorrows, yet we considered him stricken by God, smitten by him, and afflicted.

5 But he was pierced for our transgressions, he was crushed for our iniquities; the punishment that brought us peace was upon him, and by his wounds we are healed.

6 We all, like sheep, have gone astray, each of us has turned to his own way; and the LORD has laid on him the iniquity of us all.

Isaiah 6:8-10 . . . .

8 Then I heard the voice of the Lord saying, *"Whom shall I send? And who will go for us?"* **And I said,** *"Here am I. Send me!"*

9 He said, *"Go and tell this people: "'Be ever hearing, but never understanding; be ever seeing, but never perceiving.'*

10 *Make the heart of this people calloused;* m*ake their ears dull and close their eyes.*

Otherwise they might see with their eyes, hear with their ears, u*nderstand with their hearts, and turn and be healed."*

Psalms 78 :2 . . . . I will open my mouth in a parable; I will utter dark sayings of old,

Psalms 69;4 . . . . Those who hate me without a cause are more than the hairs of my head; Those who would destroy me are powerful, being wrongfully my enemies; What I did not steal, I then have to restore.

Psalms 118:22 . . . . The stone which the builders rejected Has become the chief corner stone.

Isaiah 6;10; 29:13; 53:1 . . . . Make the heart of this people fat, and make their ears heavy, and shut their eyes; lest they see with their eyes, and hear with their ears, and understand with their heart, and convert, and be healed.

Wherefore the Lord said, Forasmuch as this people draw near [me] with their mouth, and with their lips do honour me, but have removed their heart far from me, and their fear toward me is taught by the precept of men:

Who hath believed our report? and to whom is the arm of the LORD revealed?

Isaiah 62:11 . . . . Behold, the LORD hath proclaimed unto the end of the world, Say ye to the daughter of Zion, Behold, thy salvation cometh; behold, his reward [is] with him, and his work before him.

Zechariah 9:9 . . . . Rejoice greatly, O Daughter of Zion! Shout, Daughter of Jerusalem! See, your kingcomes to you, righteous and having salvation, gentle and riding on a donkey, on a colt, the foal of a donkey.

Psalm 118:22-26 . . . .

22 The stone the builders rejected has become the capstone;

23 the LORD has done this, and it is marvelous in our eyes.

24 This is the day the LORD has made; let us rejoice and be glad in it.

25 O LORD, save us;O LORD, grant us success.

26 Blessed is he who comes in the name of the LORD. From the house of the LORD we bless you. [a]

Zechariah 13:7 . . . . Awake, O sword, against my shepherd, against the man who is my associate, says the LORD of hosts. Strike the shepherd that the sheep may be dispersed, and I will turn my hand against the little ones.

Zechariah 11:12-13 . . . . 12 I told them, "If you think it best, give me my pay; but if not, keep it." So they paid me thirty pieces of silver.

13 And the LORD said to me, "Throw it to the potter"-the handsome price at which they priced me! So I took the thirty pieces of silver and threw them into the house of the LORD to the potter.

Psalm 41:9 . . . . Even my close friend in whom I trusted, Who ate my bread, Has lifted up his heel against me.

Isaiah 53:9 . . . .

9 His grave was assigned with wicked men,Yet He was with a (Q)rich man in His death,Because He had done no violence,Nor was there any deceit in His mouth.

Psalm 69:21 . . . . They also gave me gall for my food And for my thirst they gave me vinegar to drink.

Psalm 22:18 . . . . [18]They part my garments among them,

And upon my vesture do they cast lots.

Psalms 22:1 . . . . My God, my God, why hast thou forsaken me?

Psalms 31:5 . . . . Into your hands I commend my spirit; you will redeem me, LORD, faithful God.

Zechariah 12:10 . . . . And I will pour upon the house of David, and upon the inhabitants of Jerusalem, the spirit of grace and of supplications: **and they shall look upon me whom they have pierced,** and they shall mourn for him, as one mourneth for his only son, and shall be in bitterness for him, as one that is in bitterness for his firstborn

Psalms 22:16 . . . . Dogs have surrounded me; a band of evil men has encircled me, they have pierced my hands and my feet.

Psalms 22:18 . . . . They divide my garments among them, And for my clothing they cast lots.

Psalms 22:1 . . . . My God, my God, why hast thou forsaken me? why art thou so far from helping me, and from the words of my roaring?

Psalms 31 :5 . . . . Free me from the net they have set for me, for you are my refuge.

AND FINALLY, FROM THE NEW TESTAMENT: Revelation 22:16-21 . . . . 16 "I, Jesus, have sent my angel to give you[a] this testimony for the churches. I am the Root and the Offspring of David, and the bright Morning Star."

17 The Spirit and the bride say, "Come!" And let him who hears say, "Come!" Whoever is thirsty, let him come; and whoever wishes, let him take the free gift of the water of life.

18 I warn everyone who hears the words of the prophecy of this book: If anyone adds anything to them, God will add to him the plagues described in this book. 19And if anyone takes words away from this book of prophecy,

God will take away from him his share in the tree of life and in the holy city, which are described in this book.

20 He who testifies to these things says, "Yes, I am coming soon." Amen. Come, Lord Jesus.

21 The grace of the Lord Jesus be with God's people. Amen.

Jeremiah 17:5-8

5 Thus says the LORD: "Cursed *is* the man who trusts in man And makes flesh his strength, Whose heart departs from the LORD.

6 For he shall be like a shrub in the desert, And shall not see when good comes, But shall inhabit the parched places in the wilderness, *In* a salt land *which is* not inhabited.

7 "Blessed *is* the man who trusts in the LORD, And whose hope is the LORD.

8 For he shall be like a tree planted by the waters, Which spreads out its roots by the river, And will not fear[a] when heat comes;But its leaf will be green, And will not be anxious in the year of drought, Nor will cease from yielding fruit.

What is so incredible about all of these Prophecies and there are more is that they are the complete story of Jesus' life. It's main features, events, and incidents even in minute detail. All of this is plainly foretold in the Old Testament. The Old Testament was written several thousand years earlier and the Prophecies did indeed occur.

These Prophecies and occurrences are certainly much more than astonishing. They are evidence of a mind that surely transcends the capability of our human minds.

All of this brings me back to the Monks at St. Joseph's Abby. The Monks simply stated that the only reason that we are here is to get there . . . . Eternity. And we will all get there one way or another. The Big question that we are in control of is; Where are we going? To Heaven or Hell.

It surely and certainly seems time to me that we start paying attention to the instructions that we have been given. Our free wills have in the past and continue to take us in the wrong direction.

I personally tried to go my own way and do my own thing for most of my life. Fortunately for me, I had an interruption in that way of thinking and living. That interruption gave me the time and opportunity to look at life. I certainly hope that we all don't need an interruption to wake up.

EPILOGUE

The old Cherokee Chief:

One evening an old Cherokee Chief told his grandson about a battle that goes on inside people. He said, "My son, the battle is between two "wolves" inside us all. One is Evil. It is anger, envy, jealousy, sorrow, regret, greed, arrogance, self-pity, guilt, resentment, inferiority, lies, false pride, superiority, and ego. The other is Good. It is joy, peace, love, hope, serenity, humility, kindness, benevolence, empathy, generosity, truth, compassion and faith." The grandson thought about it for a minute and then asked his grandfather: "Which wolf wins?" The old Cherokee Chief simply replied, "The one you feed."

"The British 91st Brigade had no casualties in WWI Col. Whittlesey an American said that the reason there was no casualties was because the men and commanders of the 91st Brigade quoted the 91st Psalm daily. It is said that other similar units had very high casualty rates."

This story has been challenged to be an urban legend because the booklet of the 91st Psalm by which was distributed to the soldiers made the mistake of calling it the US ARMY 91st Brigade which had many casualties in WW1 and started the confusion about the credibiltiy. Older sources from the 50's acknowledge that it was a British, not American unit.

We would greatly appreciate any help on finding any source pertaining to this event. If you have any information please contact me at *sandichaibrown@yahoo.com.*

The following is our trail that we have researched for months all of which have produced nothing tangible:

We have all looked at sites which have the WW1 story. MOST INTERNET stories with this WW1 example give no documentation.

The documentation that we have to this point:

I. Katherine Pollard Carter: Mighty Hand of God book by Whittaker House: She contains the WWI story with a reference in her Bibliography. KPC was a journalist for years and kept excellent notes and had strong bibliographies. KPC has some sources or files that are somewhere in her estate because she was working on her research to be used as a TV documentary.

KPC names American Weekly, 21, February 1958 and the writer as Will Ouhsler (Oursler?) as her source for this story.

1. American Weekly, 1958 Hearst Corporation publication. Vol 21 Tracing down this issue. Would it source the story?

2. Will Ouhsler we assume is Will Oursler We have ordered 2 books by him to see if he quotes it in that source. Both were dead ends.

3. We have not been able to get our hands on this American Weekly 1958 story. Libraries, Hearst Foundation, Ebay have been our trails.

The American Weekly was a supplement to the Sunday newspapers published by the Hearst Corporation. It was published from 1

November 1896 to 1963. The publication featured popular illustrators on its cover, including the work of Edmund Dulac, Will Pogany and Jose Segrelles.

Katherine quotes Margaret Lee Runbeck for several stories.

Perhaps MLR carried the WW1 story since much of KPC is inspired by her. MLR does not have a bibliography in her book the Great Answer, but has other stories we need documented and is a powerful writer about God and the war. Margret wrote 30 years before KPC on this subject. I read this book and it was very good and highly recommend it, but did not have this story—it was mostly testimonies from WW2.

II. KPC says that many periodicals on both sides of the ocean carried the WW1 story of the protection of the men in the 91st Brigade who stood on Psalm 91. So we have a 1970's book with the story in what we assume as the correct form: (British unit) saying that she had many sources to choose from and that the documentation span both America and Britian.

F.L. Rawson, and the name of the book is called LIFE UNDERSTOOD. In it he wrote about the British 91st brigade. I only hoped that he would have a strong bibliography—which he doesn't.

In the book they said he wrote another book called, "How to Protect the Troops". Can't find a copy of this second title book.

We ordered an antique postcard carrying this story and we cannot read the date. It tells the story as a British regiment, quotes FL Rawson, a noted engineer and great scientist and says that their book, "There is a safe place to Hide" we could read about these soldiers and could be purchased for a $1. (We have not located the book as of yet.) The Address for the book is Merit Publications, Dept. S-7, 300-4th Ave., New York 10, NY. The card was written to Edna Baird, Box 36, Doniphan Nebraska—with a one penny postage stamped card.

Businessreform.com has the story contested as an urban legend. However, several in the past years say that the confusion regarding the story is the cross-over of the British regiment being changed into an US Army unit.

Robert H. Reid, pastor who contradicted the urban legend claim on the internet site (above) seems knowledgeable and have facts we don't. What is is source? There are 85 Robert H. Reids in Georgia and Alabama alone. Larry Klass refuted it as an urban legend and this is Robert's rebuttal following:

Reviewed by Pastor Robert H. Reid on July 8, 2006 Regarding Larry Klass's comments about there was no 91st brigade; this is true if you are referring to the U.S. Army. However, the 91st Brigade was a British unit. The 91st Brigade was a composite brigade put together in England. The story is true and it refers to a British unit and not an American!

British Documentation:

A. Secular/Military Research
    The 7th division was a Regular Army division formed after the start of the war It contained 20th, 21st, 22nd, and 91st Infantry brigades.
    91st Brigade was made up of four battalions. 1/South Staffords,2/Queens, 21/Manchester and 22/Manchesters.
    The Brigade was to advance on a battalion front. 1/South Staffords was to take the Red Line and then 22/Manchesters would move through to attack the Blue Line. 21/Manchesters was in support and 2/Queens was in reserve.
    Just before zero hour the Germans fired a defensive barrage designed to break up potential attacks. Fortunately it fell between the front and rear battalions. The brigade joined from the 30th Division in December 1915, swapping with the 21st Brigade. A number of battalions swapped to the brigade from other 7th Division brigades during the transition.

In 1984 Mr. Bayuk was diagnosed with multiple sclerosis. Two years after being diagnosed with that disease he wrote his first book "Coping and Prevailing". The book was written primarily for those newly diagnosed with the disease. The purpose and goal of the book was to insure to those newly diagnosed that they would and could still have a happy, fruitful and active life. MS would surely be a complication, however, a very manageable complication with many things that one could do to help themselves.

During the following years he also wrote "20 Years and Still Coping and Prevailing". A book explaining the alternatives and choices one could make utilizing integrative medicine, exercise, nutrition, etc. Mr Bayuk has always been anti-drug due to the experimental nature and adverse side effects of those therapies.

He also wrote "The Things That We Don't Talk About . . . or You Better Smile Through the Tears". A book about the compromising and uncomfortable circumstances that one could find themselves having with MS. From a reader:

Last nite I picked up your latest, 'The Things We don't Talk About' and have not been able to put it down. The information you give and the chronological order of your topics are superb. Can only describe it as fantastic reading.

I often myself wonder about—the higher purpose of life if there is one, but in your writings I see that whether you realize it or not . . . . you have provided information that will eventually benefit hundreds, nay thousands of lives. It will be much harder now for you to achieve a higher purpose than that !!!